AF323263

True Great Hot Shot Stories

Volume 1

Introduction

This book highlights some of the most interesting events that happened in my life, in some way like Woody Allen's Zelig or Forest Gump. The true events described in this book happened to me. Events like these may not happen often to other lives. At the end of these stories we will offer the opportunity to you to add some stories of your own to the next Hot Shot Stories book.

Ned F. Cruey

Table of Contents

Chapter 1
Alaska Winter Naval Adventures, World War II

The day after Pearl Harbor my father, Eugene Cruey, signed up for the U. S. Navy, not for the love of the Navy, but because he knew he could avoid the misery of the dog solder's life of walking followed by individual combat that waited the soon to be draftees. Entering January 2, 1942 at the Great Lakes Naval Station north of Chicago he found himself on a train to Seattle after two weeks of Basic Training. They issued no winter clothes, and put him on a ship to Sitka, Alaska, arriving in late January. He had no interest in college, but could do almost anything as evidenced by the fact that he made the second highest enlistment rank the Navy offered at that time in only four years.

The men at their base had no meat to eat that February. My father as a great shot and deer hunter from Ohio volunteered to go with a local Eskimo and find a moose to feed the Navy. He shot one moose but it disappeared so they kept looking. They shot another moose, cleaned it, but on their way back they found the first moose. By Eskimo rule and by the rules of any hunter, you must take any animal you shoot. My father and his Eskimo guide cleaned and carried through the deep snow both large animals out of the woods. That moose meat fed the Navy base personnel in Sitka that winter.

The U. S. Navy gave my father his own PT type boat, like JFK's, to take a small crew and patrol for the anticipated upcoming Japanese invasion. Because of the thick fog blanketing the area in the Alaskan winter, the men could not see Japanese military nearby. However, if the U.S. had not had a military presence there the Japanese would have taken that land.

No invasion came. In the winter and spring of 1941, in his PT boat my father patrolled the central Alaskan coastline but in the heavy fog they never found Japanese naval forces. Simultaneously, Hitler prepared to invade the Soviet Union. In England, Alan Turing had efforts underway to break the German Radio Code. Hitler invaded the Soviet Union on June 22, 1941, still a national day in Russia. Alan Turing broke the German code that week. Turing and Winston Churchill, the English Prime Minister, had to decide based on a mathematical formula devised by Turing which German convoys to attack to avoid alerting the Germans to the compromise of their code.

The ultimate Hot Shot, Alan Turing went on to invent the computer. Steve Jobs, the principal founder of Apple Computers, Inc., and another great Hot Shot, in the ultimate homage to Alan Turing named his company "Apple," using as the company logo the famous apple with a bite taken out of it. Alan Turing committed suicide by biting into an apple laced with cyanide.

The breaking of the German code helped the Soviets to beat and capture the German troops by intercepting all radio transmissions. They leaked the information that they always knew where and when to attack because they had Soviet spies in the German high command. In order to obtain a complete Nazi collapse, the Allies never targeted Hitler personally as victory could come about only by invasion and not by conditional surrender.

Chapter 2
In the Early Years
How to Really Stand Out from the Crowd

When my father got out of the Navy in 1946 he went to Toledo, Ohio, and started going to dances to meet girls. My mother, at 18, had recently graduated from high school in Tiffin, Ohio. She had moved to Toledo to work as a secretary. She lived in a boarding house for young women called Flower Esther. She had just accepted a secretarial job to start in Washington in two weeks when a friend asked her to go with her to a Wednesday night dance on September 19, 1946. For the first and only time, she went to the dance hall that evening. She met my father at that dance. He took her on a date to Detroit the next weekend, her first trip out of Ohio. They married on November 10, 1946. My mother gave birth to me, their only child, the following September 2nd.

With his skills in construction, my father made his living initially by repairing burned out homes in Toledo. Because of sparse housing after the war, we lived in a trailer until my parents purchased a 50-year old duplex after a year. We had a cabin cruiser on Lake Erie. From those early years in Ohio, I remember most playing with buckeyes in the summer and playing in the snow in the winter. I especially remember staying inside a lot because of the cold and snow which contributed to my many illnesses, mostly colds.

My first words, "Car car, go go, bye bye," have not changed since. So far, I have visited 150 countries throughout the world.

The cold winters in Ohio contrasted dramatically with growing up in warm South Florida, starting at age six, where kids played outside almost all their free time. In 1953, after two trips to South Florida, my parents and I moved to Fort Lauderdale because of the building boom in Florida and the need to escape the brutally cold Ohio winters.

In 1956 after we moved to Pompano Beach, we had a cabin cruiser for ocean fishing on a canal in the back yard.

My father, a hot shot in his own day, had great skills as a fisherman, hunter, and golfer. In 1961 the year Roger Maris broke Babe Ruth's home run record, he and Mickey Mantle while on baseball spring training for the New York Yankees in Fort Lauderdale, wanted to play golf. They called Sunrise Country Club where my father had become vice president. As a par golfer, my father got to play golf with the superstars.

At age eight, I had my first business. A couple of neighbors offered me $2 per week to mow their lawn. After that I knocked on the doors of all the neighbors for many blocks around to solicit more lawn jobs, with some including watering for an extra $4 per week. I could make $12 on a Saturday. I used to put the lawn mower in a wagon, attach the wagon to my bicycle, and bicycle off to the lawn mowing jobs.

By 1957 my father had done so well in his building/plastering business that every summer the three of us took off for Sault Ste. Marie, Canada, for three months to get away from the South Florida summer heat. Every year for 12 years, we three traveled through the local highways, often on mountainous roads, pre Interstate, seeing the Old South mature. Orlando had three traffic lights in the 1950s.

We had two small fishing/speed boats at our lake summer home that at age nine, I could use alone. This resulted in my only spanking after I came back with the boat one hour late after my father had told me that he had a date to go fishing at a certain time with three other men. Peer pressure resulted in my spanking.

I heard of a summer camp, Camp Waconda, across the lake. I managed to go. Like the other kids in South Florida I learned to swim and dive at an early age. My fellow campers who lived in cold weather most of the year had less experience with swimming. I became the best camper in diving and swimming, a big deal for a not-so-much-of-a-jock type kid. We visited the home on the lake for a total of four summers and I went to summer camp each year.

At age nine, I had a seven-year-old friend, small for his age, in Pompano Beach who had 16-foot speedboat in his back yard canal. His father owned a grocery store. The two of us went everywhere around the Florida Gulf Coast on the canal and intercoastal waterways in that 16- foot speedboat with a 30 horsepower Evinrude engine. We loved to race by the big ships. That may have gotten the attention of the Harbor Patrol in Port Everglades, who stopped the two of us in my friend's boat. They didn't have age laws so they had to let us go.

For my tenth birthday my father gave me a pair of boxing gloves, and friends from all over came to box with me. I had to get good at it to survive. Many of my friends came down to Pompano and Fort Lauderdale for several months in the winter and enrolled in private schools. We used to have BB gun wars in the various construction projects. We would wear heavy clothes and goggles. We had a lot of fun.

In late 1959 I went out for basketball and got on a team which won all the games. When they played the county All Stars they won 26 to 25. I played worse than any other player on the first string, but I played the whole game and I scored one point.

In the fall of 1960 I went out for football in Lighthouse Point, the first town north of Pompano. Once again we won all our games and played and beat the county All Stars, 7 to 6. I played every minute of this football game, the greatest game ever played, as I like to call it these many years later. In the summer of 2015 at my 50th reunion with Northeast High School in Fort Lauderdale, I reminisced with the quarterback of the opposing team for that game, 55 years after the game.

At that point I had never lost a game and as it turned out that ended up my only season in basketball and football, undefeated. Just as the county All Star game concluded in late October 1960 my parents sold their home on the water and moved back to Fort Lauderdale to build their first apartment house.

I transferred schools literally the day Kennedy got elected, two months into the school year in eighth grade. I got mostly Bs at school and my new school had an opening in the advanced class. After a great debate and my volunteering I entered the advanced class, a new concept for me. As it turned out the jocks/in crowd at the new school, on the losing side of the recent championship football game, knew of my recent football experience. They encouraged me to run for student council several weeks after arriving. Not really knowing anyone I came in first alternate, but shortly afterward one of the top ten winners transferred to a private school, so I got in.

Soon I became the MC at school dances and became a leader in the in crowd. My mother and I counted 24 parties that eighth grade year. The in crowd would hang out at the private Ocean Beach Club. While hanging around that Easter break, talking about the next party, I announced that my parents had left me home alone because they took our hunting dog to Northern Florida for training. I suggested we have a party in my family's apartment at my parents' fully occupied apartment building. The girls called around and over 100, thirteen year olds showed up, one quarter of the student body, a record that probably still holds. When my parents got back, the neighbors told my parents about the party. Otherwise they never would have known because we left the apartment perfectly clean after the party.

The next August as I practiced to go out for Quarterback, I kept knocking a bone spur on my left knee. The orthopedic surgeon recommended surgery. So much for football that season.

I bought a Cushman Motor scooter that August since I would turn 14 on September 2nd . I drove to my first day of 9th grade which started that day.

Five days later, the first weekend with wheels, I drove to Key West. I got a sunburn. I also observed the military buildup happening on the highway to Key West with the Cuban missile crisis forming.

The following weekend I drove to Miami to see my first concert, Roy Orbison and Paul Petersen.

The third weekend with wheels I drove to Palm Beach where I saw the excitement of President Kennedy's secret service entourage by his father's mansion, one of the houses in Palm Beach on the ocean. I had last seen him at the previous New Year's Day Orange Bowl after he had gotten elected but before he took office. Everybody said, "Where's Jackie?" Everybody assumed that he must have had his secretary sitting next to him at the Orange Bowl. Forty years later I learned the identity of the woman sitting next to him: Judith Campbell Exner, his girlfriend he shared with the Mafia boss. Who knew?

So much for my first month with a motor scooter.

Having bought my Cushman and everything else with my lawn mowing business money, I found myself in the in crowd without playing football and dead broke.

My father in the navy.
He made the highest rank in 4 years.
Eugene E. Cruey

My parent's first date in Detroit
1946

My parent's wedding day
November 10, 1946

Havana, Cuba

Family at Fort
Lauderdale
Beach

First Grade
starts soon
1953

Floyd Cruey -
Grandfather

Margaret - Mother

Mary Cruey -
Grandmother

We caught Marlin
off of our ocean
going boat
1955

Backyard Pompano Beach
1956

One of my two boats in Canada

Camp Waconda
Ontario
1957-1960

Adult party at summer camp
Lake McCarroll
1958

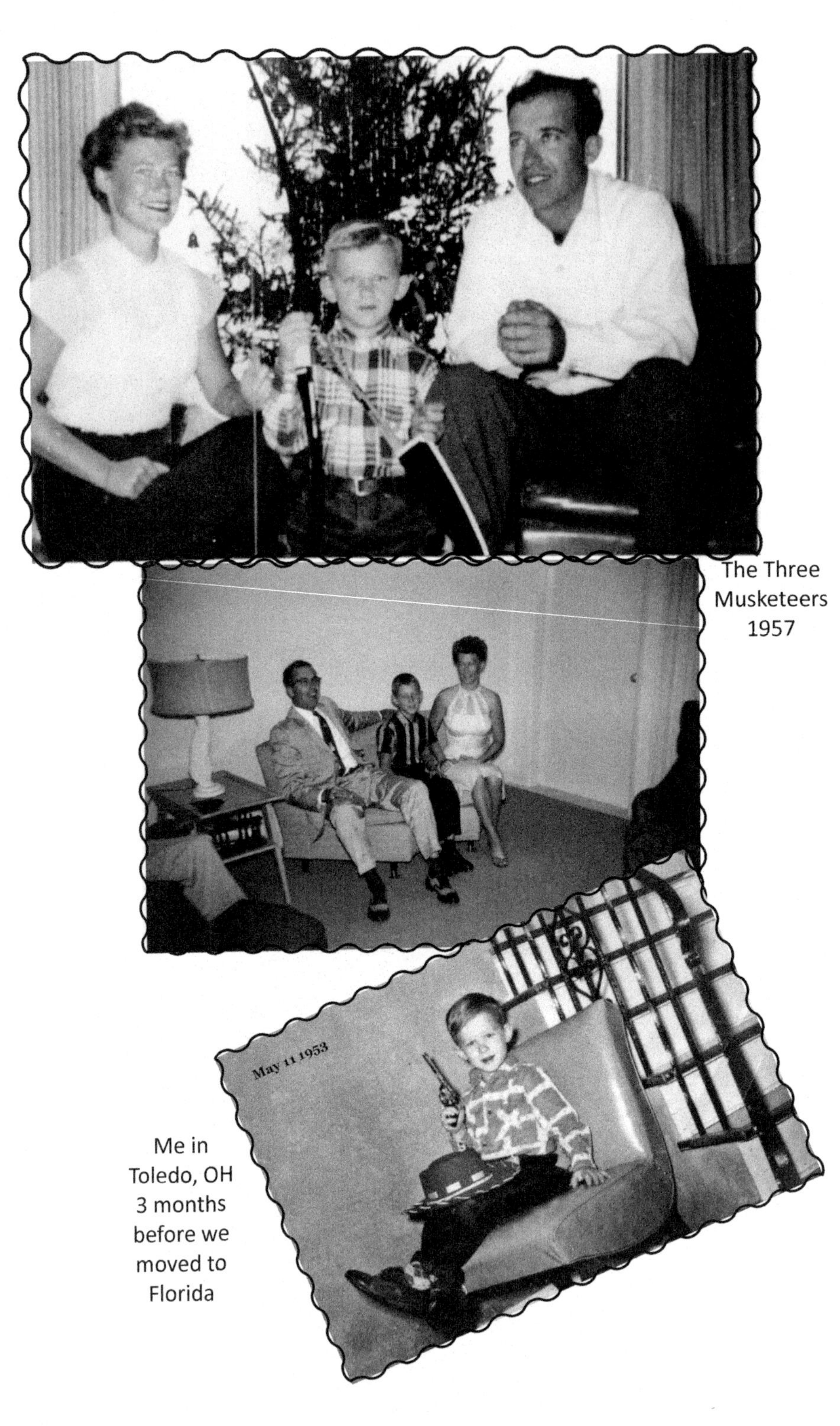

The Three
Musketeers
1957

Me in
Toledo, OH
3 months
before we
moved to
Florida

Age 8
Just started my lawn mowing business
Pompano Beach
1957

Picnic at our home at Lake McCarroll
Summer 1960

Riding horses with my mother
1958

Horse racing
Tennessee
Age 10

This picture helped my interest in becoming president
1964

Chapter 3
The Entrepreneur in the High School Years

A neighbor had a paper route for the Miami Herald and since my parents' $0.50 per week allowance didn't go far, I felt motivated enough to try a 50 customer paper route. Most of my old lawn customers lived in Pompano Beach, too far to go.

Very rarely does a cool kid have a paper route. I saw potential and within a few months I had several more routes. I bought a golf cart, put wooden sides on it, and obtained even more routes. You couldn't drive a car by yourself until 16 in Florida. All of a sudden I had all the money you could spend as a kid. Next season I had an excuse not to play football. I joined the newly formed Key Club when all the movers and shakers of my high school joined.

During the summer of my fifteenth year the Key Club had a convention that July in Pittsburg, stopping in Washington DC, and New York City, costing $200. Among all my classmates, only I could afford to go. Except for me still age 15, the other 2000 boys from around the country had already turned 16. That summer Bill Clinton, one year older than me, arranged to get photographed with JFK on one of these trips. When we got there JFK had gone out of town, so no meeting. Our principle chaperone and our U. S senator, Senator Hollings, felt very annoyed that we did not get to meet the president.

At the July 1963 Key Club convention in Pittsburgh of 2000, 16-year-old boys in attendance, for the final entertainment show I invited two of the most beautiful girls from the front desk of the Key Club convention to join me as my dates although no one else had dates. The girls agreed. My friend, the president of the Student Council at Miami

High School, arranged to save three seats in the front row. With all of the other attendees already seated in the auditorium waiting for the show to start, I walked down the center aisle with one girl on each arm and sat between them in the front row for the show.

I wondered then if I could become President.

That September, I turned 16 and bought an Oldsmobile Super Sport plus a Sprite convertible. The Olds helped me to expand my paper route business over the next three years to 750 customers. All of a sudden I realized that I made three times my teachers' pay. I had nine months to go to my first summer vacation with a car which by then turned into a VW bug as it actually worked better for my 55 mile paper route.

One of my friends who came down at Easter from Howe Military Academy in Indiana scheduled his summer to travel with me to Canada and the World's Fair in NYC. The day before I left he called to say his mother wouldn't let him go. She said it was too dangerous. I couldn't chance my parents forbidding me to go so I said nothing and took off, with all summer and unlimited money to see North America at age 16. By the way this same boy whose mother would not let him go on the trip with me died September 22, 1968 in Vietnam.

Nobody knew if a 16-year-old could get a motel so I took my sleeping bag. The first night heading for Chicago from Northern Florida I laid down off the road and soon woke up with ant bites. I moved down the road and tried again. I woke up startled at 5:00 am when I found myself 10 feet from an active railroad when a very loud train whistle shocked me out of my sleep. I found a hotel or motel from then on. I never really liked camping out. I could pull this trip off because I hired three boys to deliver my newspapers for a summer job while I billed my customers. I made more money away than they made staying home all summer.

After visiting my old summer home on the lake in Canada in June 1964, I went on to Ottawa where I sat in for one hour of a Canadian parliament final debate where they voted in the maple leaf as the Canadian flag.

I went on to tour Montreal where at 16 you could go to nightclubs. Later I went to Quebec and Gaspe. Coming down thru Maine, Massachusetts, Cape Cod, and Connecticut I ended up in New York City in late June 1964.

Because the 1964-1965 World's Fair had just started, the hotels in

New York City had become extremely expensive so I went up to Harlem and got a room for three weeks at the Charles Hotel at 123rd Street and Lexington. In those three weeks I saw all the expos at the Flushing World's Fair and I saw every play on Broadway from the front row of each one. In one of those plays, "Hamlet," I saw Richard Burton play the lead role. After the play, I saw his wife, Elizabeth Taylor, pick him up in a limousine. The police had closed down the entire street for that event. What a great time.

In Harlem a police officer stopped me for running a yellow light at a stoplight that went directly from green to red. The cop called headquarters to find out what to do with a 16 year old who had a Florida license. New York did not issue driver's licenses until age 18. The officer let me go without a ticket. I could get into nightclubs in Greenwich Village. Driving back from New York I stopped in Atlantic City and in Washington, DC.

The month after I left Harlem, they had the 1964 Harlem riots. In Washington, D.C., I stepped out of the tourist line at the Capitol and stayed three hours without interruption in the balcony in the U. S. Senate. I saw Senators Fulbright, Humphrey, and Javits in action, quite thrilling for me.

I got back to Fort Lauderdale, took back my paper routes, and started my senior year as I turned 17. I had only two regrets in high school: (1) I never ate lunch in the cafeteria as I always went out to restaurants and (2) I did not go out for schools plays. Later in life I dated actresses who sent me to acting lessons. I missed a chance to see if I had any talent early.

In my senior year I started going to college dances at the beach of the type shown in the movie, "Where the Boys Are" in Fort Lauderdale, during spring break.

With graduation coming I had planned a grand trip to Mexico and all over the west.

My parents apartment house
Volkswagon is good for delivering 750 daily
newspapers for the Miami Herald and several
grand trips

Photo Caption for Key West 1961

On my Cushman motor scooter at age 14 years 1 month old, purchased with my lawn mowing money on August 3, 1961, the day of Barak Obama's birth. I practiced for a month and got my license at age 14. Five days after I got my license, on a weekend I drove 220 miles each way to Key West and back, observing the military convoys on the highway to Key West in the buildup prior to the Cuban Missile Crisis 13 months later.

Photo Caption for Orange Bowl 1961

Joe Namath took Alabama to victory at the Orange Bowl on January 1, 1961. President elect JFK attended the game with Judith Campbell Exner. We all wanted to see Jackie and wondered, "Why would you bring your secretary to a football game?"

My undefeated team 1960, 3rd from the left, back row

Chapter 4
A Creepy Escape from Houston

The day after high school graduation I left for New Orleans. In several days I found myself in downtown Houston.

At dinner while eating in a diner I spotted two men in their early 20's and asked them where teenagers hang out. They told me they planned to go to a club and asked if I could give them a ride.

As I followed their directions, driving to the supposed nightclub with one of the men sitting in the back and one in the front seat of my car, after I told them I planned to travel to Acapulco then out west for the summer, the man sitting in the back seat started singing the Elvis song "It's now or never."

It dawned on me that they planned to rob me. I immediately suggested we all go down to Galveston the next day. Since I had already checked in at the Hilton we should leave the next morning. They must have realized that it would make a cleaner crime if they got me when I did not have a connection to a hotel. I told them, "Pick me up at 5:00 am so we have a full day there. We'll drive in my car." I dropped them off back at the diner. I went back to my hotel and I got up and left at 4:00 am.

I did not think about it for thirty years until I read an article about the conviction of two men in Houston for procuring teenage boys to a third party. Officials found at least 20 teenage boys dead and buried in this third party's back yard. It had gone on for at least 30 years. I wonder if this kind of issue may account for part of the large missing persons list in this country.

Chapter 5
The Jet Set and 18 Days in Mexico

After spending the next night in Monterrey, I went on to Mexico City, Veracruz, and then to Acapulco, the Jet Set capital of the world in 1965. The next 10 days changed my life. I stayed at the Hilton in the center of the Acapulco Bay area where somehow the young 20 somethings gathered and I got invited for dinner with the group. What a group! I met people going down to Portillo, Chile to ski in July. I also met English royalty, a beautiful singer from Germany, a 21- year-old New York City model, and a beautiful playgirl from Aspen and La Jolla. I dated the 21- year-old model from New York City. She told me that everyone should live in Manhattan at some time in their life, a thought I remembered when I graduated from USC six years later. We all ate out together and partied at the discos all night long, with romance on the beach.

I had my first social interaction with a medical doctor, me still a paperboy from Fort Lauderdale. A young new medical doctor on honeymoon at the Hotel Las Brisas, where JFK also honeymooned, came to me to fix him up to cheat on his new wife with one of the available beauties in our crowd. It blew me away. Did I mention that before this trip I had ordered by mail a Harvard sweatshirt? This did not hurt for self-promotion for a seventeen year old. I could have gone there but just did not have time.

Every night for 10 days we ate dinner at the same fabulous restaurant where we sat at one long, rectangular table with space for 15 or 20 people. As my first experience with drinking wine, we drank red wine out of bota bags.

When we all picked a date to leave Acapulco I made plans to meet my New York model girlfriend, Gail, later in Las Vegas. She had a red Mustang convertible with Florida plates. Naively, I figured that I could find her car easily in one of the casino parking lots in Las Vegas.

Of the group leaving Acapulco, a 21 year old Aspen-La Jolla playgirl, Shirley, needed a ride back to La Jolla, California, where her parents lived. We all decided that I should take her. She boasted of having affairs in Aspen with all the Kennedy men. As a 17 year old I never thought about such talk.

On a road with no fences, just 15 miles north of Acapulco, a bull ran in front of my car. It remains a mystery today how I missed him. I had shut my eyes while preparing for a crash as I slammed on the brakes. When I opened my eyes again, somehow the bull had disappeared.

The first night out of Acapulco, after eating some tainted chicken, my traveling companion, Shirley, became ill with repeated vomiting. She vomited for hours, retching all night, in a motel in the middle of nowhere on the western part of Mexico. At the time I wondered what I would do with a dead body in my car, considering the Mexican laws. Fortunately, Shirley's symptoms diminished and stopped.

The second night out of Acapulco, we stayed in a good hotel in a city along the way. Some well to do guests in their forties staying in the hotel invited us to attend their party. Within an hour I realized that several of the men present tried to get us both drunk, and had impure motives towards Shirley. I got Shirley out of there, we went to our own hotel room, and got some sleep before getting back on the road in the morning.

The trip back to the U.S. Border from Acapulco took four days of driving. Two nights after Shirley's episode of food poisoning, and the third night out of Acapulco, we could find no place to sleep and pulled off the road in a small town, asking if they could find us a place to sleep. I paid some people for the place they gave us to sleep, a room with a single bed that we shared. In the morning, we woke up to discover that they had put us up in a tortilla factory, with tortillas drying everywhere all around us. It took several days to get the smell of drying tortillas out of my nose.

We crossed the border from Mexico into Arizona just before the Fourth of July weekend.

Chapter 6
A Grand Tour of the West

When we got to Las Vegas, on July 4, 1965, I did not find the red Mustang convertible with Florida plates belonging to my model girlfriend Gail in a casino parking lot as I thought I would. Since I could not find Gail in Las Vegas, I invited Shirley to go with me on a grand tour of the entire west coast before taking her back to La Jolla.

In Las Vegas, Shirley and I went to a nightclub in the Thunderbird where we could dance, as long as we did not get too close to the gaming tables.

While having my car serviced, I walked around old downtown Las Vegas. I spotted smoke coming out of a closed auto body shop. The only time in my life, I got to pull the fire alarm on the street down the block. Fire engines arrived in five minutes and fire fighters put out the fire.

One of the most interesting events of this several week trip within a trip occurred late at night when we pulled off the road to get a little sleep in my car. After a couple of days enjoying Las Vegas, we left there one night at about 10:00 pm to continue our trip. We drove for a few hours until we reached Provo, Utah, after 2:00 am. When we pulled off the road to get a few hours rest, we inadvertently parked in Lovers Lane. At 5:00 am the police knocked on the window. They asked for ID and for the first time I admitted my age, 17 years 10 months old. The police took us to the station to check us out. They tried to call my parents but with my parents traveling to Alaska, the officers could reach no one. They determined that I had no warrants out for my arrest, that my car had insurance, and that the car belonged to me. I checked out ok. All of the officers from the night shift as well as all of the officers from the just-starting day shift came by to see us. Every one of the police officers shook my hand.

Shirley and I left Provo and drove all over the west including British Columbia, Glacier National Park, Yellowstone, the Seattle Space Needle, and down the scenic Oregon coast to the California coast, all the way to La Jolla. I met Shirley's parents and saw their beautiful home when I dropped Shirley off.

After leaving Shirley I went to LA where I discovered an automatic newspaper folding machine which I had shipped to Fort Lauderdale to save time and money on my paper route for my employees who folded my newspapers every morning.

After visiting Ohio and Washington D.C., to look up a girl I had met the previous summer, I drove home to Fort Lauderdale.

Chapter 7
High Adventure in the Caribbean at 18

At the end of the summer I prepared to go to Broward Junior College and continue my 750 customer newspaper route. It turned out Broward Junior College had the best professors in the U.S., all retired Ivy League superstars teaching one course per semester.

On November 7, 1965, my parents sold their apartment building. Three days later on November 10th , their wedding anniversary, they moved to California.

Suddenly on my own at age 18, I rented space in a house in the area. Keep in mind that for the past four years I had made three times more money than my teachers with no living expenses.

That Christmas break, December 1965, I hired substitutes to deliver my papers and took off for a two-week trip throughout the Caribbean.

First I went to Jamaica where I rented a car and drove on the left side of the road for the first time. I drove all over Jamaica. It became part of my résumé later on that I had experience driving on the left side of the road.

After several days I caught a night flight to Haiti, where Papa Doc the Voodoo dictator, remained in power at the time. I met someone my age on the plane to Haiti, on his way to visit his uncle, the Austrian ambassador, for Christmas holiday. He invited me to join him at his uncle's home for several days. I accepted. When we arrived we left the plane and entered Haitians customs together. It turned out that U. S. President Lyndon Johnson, the month before had sent undercover agents to infiltrate and possibly overthrow Papa Doc. My new travel companion participated in ROTC at his Eastern College and had a book with him regarding that course that had pictures of various guns. Since no one from the Haitian customs could read English, they took both of us under guard with 15 soldiers to the Port au Prince police station where we spent four hours in Papa Doc's jail from midnight to 4:00 am before my friend's uncle, the ambassador, could get us out. We went to the Austrian ambassador's beautiful residence up in the hills to spend the rest of the night. They took me on a tour of Port au Prince the next day. I had a great 24 hours in Haiti, but I took the next plane out to Puerto Rico, feeling happy to get out of there.

On arriving in San Juan, Puerto Rico I took a day trip to the city of Ponce on the público, which consists of a car that holds six passengers with three in the front and three in the back, through the mountains of central Puerto Rico to the other side of the island, where you might sit next to someone holding a chicken on their lap.

In San Juan, I stayed on the casino strip at the Caribe Hilton where I met other teenagers mostly from New York City on Christmas vacation with their parents. We all hung out and visited the various casinos together. One night we all stayed up playing Black Jack. When the casinos closed at their mandatory closing time at 4:00 am, I suggested to my teenage friends, all of whom had plenty of money, that they join me in my room and I would deal Black Jack. We all went to my room and I made $600 dealing black jack in my room at $10 a hand. I wonder how many rules we broke.

Chapter 8
Loss of My Empire, the Greatest Spring Break Ever,
And Moving On

When I returned to Fort Lauderdale after New Year's 1966 I learned that one of my paperboy employees got sick and the branch manager had to help deliver half of the papers. He had just gotten married and needed the money so he completed a coup against my empire, cutting my newspaper route in half.

I had planned to do two years at Broward Junior College, two years at Florida Atlantic College, followed by three years at the University of Miami law school, all funded by my newspaper delivery business.

Since my parents had moved to the San Diego area I decided to make a complete break and join them after the next semester. I signed up to have all my classes on Tuesday and Thursday so I would have plenty of free time during the upcoming six-week spring break in Fort Lauderdale, from early March to late April. During spring break, I did my homework at the beach.

Right after I had lost half of my paper routes, I learned that the people I had rented space in their home from received the news that their only child had just accidentally killed himself while cleaning his weapon in Fort Benning, GA, and they needed my space for his widow and infant. I got two weeks' notice to move out. I found a house where I could rent a room, a real party scene that had many other college kids staying there while on spring break. Between the college visitors from the north and the parties with the other residents I had a blast that semester while delivering my smaller paper route. As a result I had college friends all over the Midwest and East to visit later. As a concept new to me, I met members of top, super cool fraternities at big universities.

I left Fort Lauderdale for San Diego on May 1, 1966, finally with no paper route to help keep me flush for money for the first time. My paper routes had given me my financial life line for 4 ½ years.

When I arrived in San Diego on May 5th I immediately went to Ensenada, Mexico, 100 miles away, for the Cinco de Mayo celebration activities. Thanks to a new concept, computer dating, I had five dates lined up in San Diego, from May 7th through May 19th. In between the previously scheduled computer-dating dates, I took off for Las Vegas to obtain 600 Kennedy half dollars at Caesars' Palace because I heard you could sell them in Europe for four dollars each.

I put my car up for sale, sold it, and purchased a one way ticket to England on the ship, SS Berlin, leaving New York City on June 9th on a nine-day Atlantic crossing. On May 20th my father drove me to the eastern outskirts of San Diego and dropped me off with my very heavy Samsonite suitcase containing 600 Kennedy half dollars, which did not have wheels, with wheels for suitcases not invented for 30 more years.

Chapter 9
Four Continents in 124 Days on a Motorcycle

What a hitchhiking experience! I waited less than five minutes for my first ride on the outskirts of San Diego. I met a Marine on leave also hitching east at a truck stop in New Mexico. We asked a trucker if we could ride in the back of the open truck. Riding throughout the night we felt grateful to use some heavy coats they had so we traveled outdoors warm. The next day we got a ride to Kansas with someone who wanted to sleep while we drove his car. However, his car had no high gear. We drove all night in 3rd gear.

I got to southern Indiana in 40 hours where I called one of my new girlfriends I had met at spring break that spring in Fort Lauderdale. After a visit she took me up to the Indy 500 arriving just as they had a massive crash. Graham Hill won and only 10 cars finished.

At the end of the Indy 500 race, from Indianapolis I took a Greyhound bus to visit a friend at Ohio State. Although he belonged to a top fraternity, he had to live in the freshman dorms, where I stayed with him. I got to see fraternity life as well as dorm life over 2 ½ days. When his school term finished we went up to his home in Cleveland where I had a great time with him and his friends before I eventually flew to New York on a $20 half price youth fare ticket.

I get on the SS Berlin June 9, 1966 for a nine day Atlantic crossing to England, an experience which would change my life. That year, any and all college kids going to Europe for the summer traveled by ship, for the last time. The following years 98% traveled by airplane. Students among the passengers included 150 college girls, 30 guys, and me, a great ratio for a guy. UCLA had accepted me to start my sophomore year there. I became a California boy who had spent three weeks of his life in California.

On the ship I met a couple of 22 to 24 year old guys. One had just earned a MBA from USC and the other had one more semester to go to get an undergraduate degree in Business Administration also from USC, a school I had never heard of at the time. I only knew of UCLA as in the beautiful part of Los Angeles and as one of the California state schools. In those days to get a business degree as an undergrad you could only go to a private university.

Every night we partied until breakfast. What a blast! The three of us bonded and made superficial plans to start a conglomerate corporation after we all finished our education. One friend agreed to travel up to Denmark with me on the motorcycle I planned to buy in London. The other friend went off to mountain climb in Switzerland. He had just inherited a half million dollars from his father, a conglomerate owner. A little side bar: when we all went swimming in the indoor swimming pool room we decided to have arm wrestling contests among the males. I had never really tested my abilities before and nobody knew I had thrown 750 daily newspapers from the sunroof of my car every day for the past five years. I beat everybody in a row, five at a time, making me the young hero. I met one girl who lived in London, Zurich, and Beirut. I stayed at her place in all three locations throughout my summer travels. Some Swedish girls invited me to Mid Summers Eve, a celebration lasting five days just outside Stockholm, starting on June 21.

We left for Sweden shortly after disembarking the ship and after I bought a motorcycle. You couldn't rent a car at age 18 so buying a motorcycle worked out. Some other college guys did this also, but usually age 21. I never heard of anyone buying a motorcycle at age 18 to tour Europe and beyond. I bought a used 500 cc Velocette, a big motorcycle for my size. I knew of the potential dangers in riding a motorcycle but I had experience riding a Cushman motor scooter for two years from age 14 to 16. I drove extremely carefully and never let another vehicle get near me all summer.

My friend and I enjoyed the Mid Summers Eve summer solstice celebration on the islands near Stockholm, a total party scene, with everything validated that I ever imagined or heard about Swedish girls.

My friend got off in Copenhagen and I went to Berlin, entering East

Germany through Checkpoint Charlie, spending time in East Germany talking to very unhappy youth stuck in their communist country.

I stopped in St. Moritz and in Zurich, Switzerland, then drove down to Cannes, France. On the way through the Alps I met a tour bus of American college girls touring Europe. They invited me to join them and I spent several hours trying to figure out how to get my heavy motorcycle on board. When we could not load my motorcycle on their bus, we said goodbye. The hotels on the French Riviera cost too much so I stayed for a week in a youth hostel, the first of two times ever, the other in Damascus. They made you clean up as you left.

I visited a French language summer school and somehow met a Norwegian girl studying French for the summer. (As a sidebar, for this upcoming summer of 2016 my twin teenage boys have enrolled in this same French language school.) She and I would go to the beach and see the U.S. Navy sailors on shore leave. We went dancing at night. Night clubbing on the French Riviera cost too much for an 18 year old so we would go in, start dancing, and dance for several hours without sitting down, to avoid having to buy a $4 drink. If you never sat down and ordered a drink you could dance free. After a week we said goodbye. I would meet her nine years later in Oslo, after she had become a dentist.

After traveling through Nice and Monaco I went on to the Leaning Tower of Pisa, Florence, and Rome. Keep in mind every night I went to the local nightclubs where other Americans in their late teens and traveling tourist would gather to meet and hang out.

After Rome I went down to Naples and took a boat with my motorcycle to Capri. I arrived in early evening and went to one of the many hotels on the island. Standing in the lobby by an incredible coincidence, I found my friend John who I had previously dropped off in Copenhagen. He had gone to Capri to visit some of the 21-year-old girls from our ship crossing. We all hung out for several days and when we made our plans for the rest of the summer John agreed to accompany me on to Greece and Egypt.

John and I took off on my motorcycle across southern Italy to board a midnight twice-a- week ship from Bari to Piraeus, the port near Athens. As it got dark my headlight burned out with three hours of night driving left. We had to make the ship by midnight or lose half a week. I could see the road only by following another vehicle all the way for two hours, all driving faster than I wanted to go, which made it a very scary ride for both of us. We arrived in Bari at 11:55 pm, asked for directions to the port, and drove straight onto the boat ramp. Before we could turn off the engine of the motorcycle, the boat pulled away from shore. The next day we arrived in Piraeus and found out that a once-a-week ship to Alexandria, Egypt, would leave in three hours. We immediately drove to Athens, got the headlight replaced, raced up to the Parthenon, and raced back to Port Piraeus to board the ship before it departed.

Arriving in Egypt, my second, third world country after Haiti, it surprised me to learn that it took six separate bribes to get my motorcycle off the ship and through customs. We took off for Cairo and the Pyramids. In Cairo I sent all my relatives postcards, the last communication that both my grandfathers ever received from me as both passed away within a year.

We scrambled my motorcycle around the Pyramids and the Sphinx getting chased by the local people as they did not allow motorcycles there. When we got back to Alexandria we found that we could get to the Middle East only by ship, with the available next ship, in that case, a Russian cruise line ship going to Cypress then Beirut.

In 1966, the height of the cold war, we came in on a Russian ship. When we arrived in Cyprus we walked around simulating mean Russians. What a hoot! In Beirut I visited my friend from the SS Berlin, and my friend John flew back to Denmark.

I set out for Jerusalem through Syria. I visited all the sights in the Holy Land. I prepared to drive back through Turkey in the heat of August. One hundred miles before reaching Istanbul it got dark. When I asked a local farmer for directions to a nearby hotel, he invited me to stay at his farm house. We exchanged addresses and when I got back to California I found my ring which I had left in his home, waiting for me.

After visiting Istanbul I set out for Bulgaria, Yugoslavia, Hungary, Austria and Czechoslovakia, on my way to Paris. Credit cards did not yet exist the way they do now and my money had started to run low, so I stayed in the Pigal section of Paris in what later I learned rented rooms to prostitutes for their work.

From Amsterdam and the Port of Rotterdam, I went to Hull, England. From there I crossed England to Liverpool. I visited the Cavern

Nightclub where the Beatles started. I took another ship to Dublin, drove to Belfast, and took another ship to Glasgow, Scotland. In Scotland, I drove to Edinburgh. I drove down England visiting Nottingham, Oxford, and Stratford on Avon.

Finally I reached London where I sold my motorcycle back to the same shop where I bought it. I bought a ticket on the SS United States leaving August 31, 1966 for New York City. I paid for the last night's hotel, bought the train ticket for the boat train to Southampton, and got on the ship with $0.75 left.

Once again on the SS United States, the ship had five times more college girls than boys on board the ship. I had my 19th birthday on the ship, dating a 21-year-old soon-to-become school teacher. I couldn't celebrate my birthday because of my much younger age than the ages of my contemporaries. The ship docked in New York City a day late because we went through a full blown hurricane in the North Atlantic.

What a beautiful experience to see waves as high as a four story building, especially since I don't get seasick. Several times, no one but me made it to dinner. I once read that the Rockefeller brothers had taken a grand trip of Europe and the same Middle Eastern countries that I visited, putting me in great company, especially since I had my only source of income from working as a paperboy. I bet I had more fun.

When the ship docked in New York City, I walked to Western Union and had my parents wire $200 to me. While heading back to California to go to college, I visited girls I had met on the trip. I arrived back in San Diego on September 24, 1966 after 124 days on the road. I spent one night at home with my parents in San Diego. The next day my father drove me to UCLA.

John and I, age 18, in Italy

Chapter 10
Volunteering for the Draft during the Vietnam War

My father and I drove by USC on the way to UCLA since my new friend, John, went to USC and I had never heard of it before my 124 day trip. Having stayed at the top frat house at Ohio State that summer I decided I should try out for only the top house at UCLA, having no second choice, backup. The Beta Theta Pi fraternity initially accepted me, but after a night of poker playing where I won most of the money, somebody blackballed me. I had to settle on renting a room off campus.

UCLA as a public university did not offer an undergraduate major in business administration. Still looking at a possible future as a lawyer, I signed up for three courses, all required for my major in pre law studies: Latin, philosophy and physical anthropology. I hated all three equally with 24-year-old teaching assistants as professors. I visited the Los Angeles Times about getting a newspaper dealership since I had gotten used to having unlimited money. They said I had wait two years to turn 21, to sign a contract. But wait, because of the military draft, even at age 21 no one could allow me to sign a legally binding contract.

Vietnam had never before entered my equation. At the height of the Vietnam War, the U.S. Government drafted young men into the Army between the ages of 18 and 26 who did not attend college. However, until completing the military service obligation, one could not sign legally binding contracts until age 27.

I realized I could solve all my problems by volunteering for the draft, to enter the U. S. Army in order to complete my military obligation.

I knew that if I got into the Army by December 5th I could get a 3 month early out to go back to college. With the GI bill helping to pay, I could go to USC, a far more expensive school, which offered an undergraduate major in Business Administration.

On the first Tuesday in November 1966, the day of Ronald Reagan's election to governor of California, I withdrew from UCLA. I drove down to my parents in San Diego and announced my plans. They felt shocked and not thrilled. Every young man entering the U. S. Army during the Vietnam War had risk of going into combat, with 600 per week dying. A total of 58,000 U.S. servicemen died during the Vietnam War. In both wars in Iraq and Afghanistan combined, 4,800 U. S. servicemen and women have died over 12 years.

I knew that under a Communist system I would never have had all my good fortune in life. Having traveled through five Communist countries already I knew I did not want to live under Communism, so I had no problem with the Army or Vietnam.

With patriotism in mind as well as the desire to solve the problem of my inability to sign contracts with the draft hanging over me, at age 19 I flew into Ft. Lauderdale to go into the Army at the Selective Service Office where I had registered the year before. A year earlier or less I never would have thought I would ever see the military.

I still see this chapter in American history as necessary to bankrupt and eventually end the Soviet Union. I still believe that had we not had the war in Vietnam, the domino theory could have kept the Soviet Union in power and existence. This war bled the Soviet Union financially, compounded by their future loss in Afghanistan, the nuclear meltdown in Chernobyl, the multiple thousands killed in Southern Russia in the early 1990's because of faulty construction Soviet style, and the final straw when the bread lines in Moscow went from twelve hours to thirteen hours. The collapse of the Soviet Union caused three people to die. The United States had spent 2/3 of the military budget annually to contain them since 1945. We Vietnam era vets played a pivotal role in stopping the Soviet Union in its tracks. Take pride in this, vets! By the way, you will not see this in print in very many other places.

An interesting side story: the week before the Soviet Union ceased to exist, Mikhail Gorbachev flew to Cuba to tell Fidel the bad news. On the way back he stopped to refuel in Spain. Spanish authorities would not let them refuel until paid in hard cash. Mr. Gorbachev waited on the tarmac many hours for a Russian plane to bring the cash, all the while in possession of the nuclear codes to literally blow up the world from his stranded plane.

Chapter 11
Basic Training and MP School
During Active Troop Buildup in Vietnam

At 6:00 am on Monday, December 5, 1966, the Selective Service Director swore me into the U. S. Army as part of the weekly group at the Selective Service Office in downtown Ft. Lauderdale, FL. They took us right to the airport and we flew immediately to Ft. Benning, Georgia, our destination for the two months of Army Basic Training. Everybody had an upbeat attitude.

Finding myself with a mixed group of fellow draftees both high school graduates and dropouts, I was determined to do well on the three days of academic testing the Basic Training program announced. Most of my fellow draftees felt really unhappy to learn that they would have three days of academic testing. I resolved to ace the tests to make up for my low social position and not attending college. I felt good about my performance on the tests. Other people commented that they had only completed part of the tests. They got our results immediately from civilian female employees. They told me I might qualify for Officer's Candidate School. I remember one woman saying to me, "Whatever you do, make sure to go back to college."

After the tests, we had our heads shaved. We walked outside between two medics who shot both of our arms simultaneously with immunizations. Basic training started at that moment. I found myself in the Deep South in a platoon directed by three Black combat infantry drill sergeants, recently returned from Vietnam. They told us that they would do us a favor, teach us what we needed to know to survive in the jungles of Vietnam.

We had some good news. Because of winter we didn't swelter like those taking training in the summer. We also had other good news, our wakeup call at 5:15 am. I had no problem with that as to deliver my newspapers I had awakened at 3:45 am six days a week and 2:30 am on Sundays for the previous five years.

Word came down that someone had gotten a 140 GT score in this collection of draftees from the nation's various ghettos and other non-descript places, with a GT score of 100 as average.

I got the GT score of 140. I had one year of college. I had always had a knack for finding the answer to complicated math problems quickly but without doing the scut work necessary for teachers to follow my process. I got the nickname, "The Gimmick," from my math teacher. To give you an idea, Al Gore got a 134 GT score after prep school and four years at Harvard when he joined the Army to become a journalist. Drill sergeants from all over the base came to see someone with such a high score.

Within a week I got the offer to have an interview for Officer Candidate School. To become an officer would have meant one extra year to my two-year obligation. I thought, well I could stay two extra years and become a captain. It wouldn't hurt to get into politics. Harry Truman became President of the U. S. as an Army Captain. They immediately convened an interview with four majors. They asked me some questions one of which I failed. I failed because my mind worked faster than their minds. They asked what I would do if I got ambushed while leading a convoy through Vietnam. I said, get the soldiers out in the ditches and shoot back. They wanted me to say, speed up, drive straight on, and don't stop. Duh, I knew that. I just assumed the ambush included having the road blocked. General York sent me a letter the next month saying that the Army did not need 19-year-olds to become officers at that time. It turned out the Infantry Second Lieutenants had the highest death rate in Vietnam over the coming years.

Individually, I dodged a bullet two weeks into basic training.

We had Christmas vacation for two weeks after closure of basic training. They encouraged everyone to go home. Since I had no hair, for social reasons I did not want to leave. I spent two weeks with the company clerks and drill sergeants. After I beat the chief company clerk out of his pay playing pool, I gave him his money back if he would excuse me from KP, kitchen police, during the coming 6 ½ weeks of basic training. This thankless job lasted 18 hours and you didn't get to learn in the training program. You could miss out on something which could cost you your life in combat.

The drill sergeants told us to shoot as accurately as possible in the rifle shooting finals and it wouldn't mean you would get straight upfront infantry, something nobody really wanted. Anyway, out of 1000 troops in my battalion I came in second. An alligator poacher from the Okefenokee swamps beat me out. Expert rifle badge for me. They seemed to gear the training for third graders.

I spent my spare time studying vocabulary lists of Germany, Italian, and French, since I already knew Spanish. Every spare moment I would study these lists. The drill sergeants gave me two extra jobs. After dinner at night they would have me meet with some of the guys having trouble learning the rules of guard duty and review the 10 rules of guard duty with them. They also had me grade scores on rifle range tests. I knew scores and I didn't fudge others' scores to give expert ratings if they didn't deserve it. The drill sergeants took me off of that duty. They wanted me to give higher-than-merited scores to make their company look well-trained.

In late January I ran up to my three Black drill sergeants, "Request permission to go to the company day room to see myself on the Dating Game." I wanted to see an airing of one of two shows I had appeared on in October while living in Los Angeles. The drill sergeants fell over laughing and said no. I never did see any of those shows but several people at my 50th anniversary high school reunion said they saw me on the Dating Game. One of the guys who won was gay and tried to get a date with me. In Basic Training they started calling me Hollywood from then on. We had gone there to learn how to survive the jungles of Vietnam, sorry.

Another memorable moment came when the Second Lieutenant in our training company asked me about the Mardi Gras in New Orleans, since I had a reputation as a world traveler. As, the Army forbids fraternization, a collection of officers had me in to ask what talk I had with the Second Lieutenant. I covered him by denying any inappropriate talk took place.

I had another interesting experience when I sprained an ankle the day before our planned 20-mile forced march with heavy backpack. I asked for permission not to go. They denied that permission but gave me an elastic bandage to wrap my ankle. I survived. Who knew you could walk 20 miles with a heavy Army backpack with a swollen ankle? The day we ended basic training 1,000 new recruits graduated from Basic, 999 got orders for AIT, advanced infantry training, the one you don't want to get, and one got Military Police training, me. I suspect it had something to do with my high GT score.

Fifteen minutes before the buses left someone told the drill sergeants that I had missed KP for two months. They literally said they felt mad about it, but they could do nothing about it. Good luck at the Military Police School and don't arrest old drill sergeants as an MP. Drill Sergeants Dudley, Taylor, and Moore were off for another group of raw recruits.

Next at MP School in Ft. Gordon, Georgia, I found almost everyone else attending belonged to RA, Regular Army, which meant you had to sign up for three years to get the special MP School. Many were sons of cops throughout America. I couldn't believe it.

I still had a dislike of cops since they use to sleep half the night and pick me off, running stop signs at 4:30 am while delivering newspapers. They would get credit toward their ticket quota and I would have ticket licensing restriction problems as a 16 or 17 year old.

I realized MP School must have benefits over infantry. Most of the MP School students, age 21 or22, had had to sign up for three years in RA (Regular Army), while I, at age 19, as a draftee had an obligation for only for two years in US (US Army).

The second day the first sergeant called me in and asked me to go into the dining room, get the MP School students' attention and give them his message. I saw this as a test to see if I could have enough presence to become an MP. I walked into that dining room and shouted as loud as I could. Everybody stopped in their tracks. No infantry for me.

Keep in mind the whole time I was in the Army, 600 men died every week in Vietnam. The same number as any week during World War II. I did the math. In MP school I got an expert badge for pistol shooting, and continued studying my language vocabulary lists. For the first time I observed that every other trainee, 59 others, in my platoon got drunk every night. That surprised me. After MP school, the entire training company of 400 men got orders for their next duty station, with all but 20 getting Vietnam.

Twenty got orders for Ft. Mac Arthur in Southern Los Angeles for guard duty at missile sites. I had expected to go to Vietnam where they allowed MP's to volunteer for helicopter gunship duty. They wanted higher IQ soldiers to man the machine guns on helicopters. I thought I could maybe stop the North Vietnamese invasion myself; I was such a good shot. Anyway they sent me to California with the group of 20 soldiers.

Chapter 12
Stateside Duty in Malibu

It turns out that they had a battery of missile sites to the north of Los Angeles. Who knew? They had the headquarters in Van Nuys about 10 miles from my old school, UCLA. They took one look at my GT score and the head of the battalion finance department had me work with him. He had a master's degree and only got a 128 to my 140. They offered me the finance department job for my entire army stint. No Vietnam. I felt tempted but he worked 13 hour days six days a week pushing papers for $100 a month pay.

I turned it down and got myself transferred to a lovely missile outpost on top of the mountains of Malibu Beach. I had duty there from April to November 1967, high season at the beach. On my first day as a MP, they issued me a pistol and told me to guard a particular soldier back in the day room. He had threatened suicide and they told me to guard him until the van arrived to transport him to Ft. Mac Arthur. I waited with him in the day room for several minutes until he picked up the fireplace poker and told me that if I didn't pull out my pistol and shoot him he would kill me with the poker. That took place during my first hour as a cop, age 19. If I shot him they would probably transfer me to infantry in Vietnam without the proper training. Things like that can happen with 600 per week dying. I walked out of the day room, locked him in, and waited outside for the transport.

For the next six months I had a blast in Los Angeles, Hollywood, and Malibu. The secret to quality of life in an army company involved avoiding the sergeants who always look for privates to assign duties to in their spare time. I use to hang out with my friend, the dentist, a major, and I would read the Los Angeles Times in his trailer. You know shades of Beetle Bailey.

I bought a used convertible sports car and rented it out to fellow soldiers on the first few days of the month after they got paid. During the first days of the month, I took the bus to the USO on Hollywood Boulevard. When my fellow soldiers ran out of money later on in the month I drove myself around Southern California. To get the missile training assignment, you had to sign up for four years, protecting the individual from Vietnam combat for concerned mothers to worry about. Assorted troops on the base waiting for orders to Vietnam felt jealous of me, a two-year man. One of the well-meaning bunk mates got drunk and told everyone he planned to fight me. One day in the mid-morning, as I slept in the barracks after the midnight shift of guard duty this soldier challenged me to fight. The whole barracks came to watch. I said no. He responded by punching me in the face with his fist. With everyone watching, I jumped up, started yelling and dove into him, screaming. I never stopped punching. They had to pull me off. I never had another fight, aside from boxing matches. I guess that football training helped. He came by the next day and wanted to become my friend—sorry Floyd Banks.

We had police dogs on our base and we needed to train them. Since I had had large dogs all my life I volunteered to put on anti-dog gear and jump out on them in training. I had fun working with the dogs. The night before my 20th birthday I drew the top of the mountain site for guard duty. A special van came up the mountain in the morning to relieve the soldier on guard in the morning. When my shift ended at 8:00 am the van arrived with six soldiers in it instead of only the driver. That seemed odd to me, on my 20th birthday, with the six soldiers coming up on the van, voluntarily, as they wanted to see my reaction when they told me that my orders came for Vietnam. I felt excited for the possible coming adventure of volunteering for helicopter machine gun duties. When we got to the base everybody came out to talk about the orders that came, nine soldiers to Vietnam and one to Taiwan, they thought. Nobody knew for sure. It took 24 hours to confirm that I had received orders for Thailand, unheard of for a draftee status soldier. At that moment I got my life back, with no more risk of becoming a statistic as one of the 600 weekly combat deaths in Vietnam.

Chapter 13
Ned's Excellent Adventure in Thailand

I reported to Oakland, California, in early December 1967, to ship out to Thailand. I learned that I would have three days hanging around the Oakland Transit Base. I watched the soldiers board the military aircraft each day by the thousands, wearing full combat gear and carrying all their equipment in duffel bags, an eerie experience. Every morning after making roll call, I had no further responsibilities until the next morning. On the first day, I called my friend who I had met on the SS Berlin the year before. In earlier decades, her father, a builder, had built most of Daly City, California. She picked me up in her new Mustang convertible. We would drive through the Bay Area out to Marin County north of San Francisco to a private airport where she kept her private airplane. We would fly around the Bay Area as well as practice her "touch and go" landing techniques. I did not suggest that she fly us under the Golden Gate Bridge. As urban legend has it, Senator John McCain, someone who I briefly met during his run for the U. S. presidency in 2008, flew his U. S. Navy fighter jet under the Golden Gate Bridge at some point before his plane got shot down in Vietnam.

After stops in Hawaii and Clark Air Force Base in the Philippines, I arrived on a commercial flight with several other military police in Bangkok on December 5, 1967, one year to date after entering the Army. We had a couple of days to ourselves before they decided where to send each of us upcountry. I walked around the world-famous Temple of Dawn featured on every world advertising photos of Bangkok, Thailand. We walked up to the upper outside sections since they had repair construction in progress, but with no one else present to stop us, we walked up. As we got higher just at the base of the dome I spotted a wire/steel throw down ladder fixed to the side of the dome. Naturally I took the ladder up. I spent half an hour on top of the dome overlooking Bangkok. I think of that day every time I see a travel poster of Thailand, as photos always include the Temple of Dawn. I finally inched my way down the ladder and we got out of there.

I received orders to go to Camp Friendship 3 ½ hours north of Bangkok, next to Korat. They had a big U. S. Airbase there for bombing Vietnam plus a smaller army contingent. When I arrived with several other replacement MPs the sergeant major took one look at my 140 GT score and invited me to join the headquarters team to assist driving the colonel around the base and the country. I asked, "Does this mean no MP duty?" He said, "You will have no MP duty. The job is what you make of it." I said, "Thank you."

Newly arrived they put me in an MP barracks with the worst bed location. I remember the first Saturday, late afternoon, with all of us off duty, I had taken a rest lying in my bunk. Four guys used the barracks phone next to my bunk, with no privacy. The next thing I knew they got in a Jeep and left. The driver came from New York. As New Yorkers don't start driving at 16 like me, at age 18, he had just gotten his Army-issued driver's license. With little experience driving, he drove a mile down the road and ran a stop sign. He and his three companions all died. The colonel became furious. We all went to the memorial service.

After about a week in the MP barracks I transferred to a two apartment duplex house at the motor pool. I had my own apartment with daily maid service, not bad for a draftee.

Two weeks after I arrived at Camp Friendship, my full coronel, our 23-year-old beautiful, married American secretary, and I went to the Bob Hope-Raquel Welch USO Show at the Korat Air Base, the only USO show that I ever saw. They waited for our arrival and did not start the show until we seated ourselves in the front row.

The next eight months, I had quite an adventure. I worked as the colonel's aide for the Special Troops Unit that had charge of all the R & R (rest and relaxation) centers for the country of Thailand, as well as security for the adjacent Air Force base. We would travel around the base and the whole country. He would bark orders and suggestions to the first sergeants. I started writing down everything he said and would review the results at later visits. As I dropped the colonel off at his house at 5:00 pm late every afternoon it freed me to drive the Army sedan anywhere I wanted. I went to downtown Korat, played poker at the airbase, went to the golf driving range, went to the movies, and went many other places.

Starting early January 1968, the University of Maryland Extension School offered eight week college courses, three credits each, two nights a week. Through an affiliation with the U. S. military, they taught at military bases throughout the world allowing military personnel to take college credit courses during their enlistment. I signed up for two courses Monday through Thursday night. I picked up 21 college credits in the coming months, including a three-credit correspondence course in literature that I took through the University of California at Berkeley, satisfying many of my required courses to get my college degree later from USC.

The Tet offensive started the end of January 1968, 300 miles away in Vietnam. That began the decline of any hope of victory in Viet Nam. My colonel, the only one I reported to, took off for Vietnam for several days. Everybody at the base spent several days and nights camping out in the ditches of Camp Friendship waiting for a possible attack. Since I did not have any assigned company and did not have an assigned weapon, I occupied myself by taking the Army sedan and picking up the only single "round eye" girl (American- or European-speak for Caucasian) who worked at the Army base. I took her to the pool for a date, while everyone else stayed in the ditches. When the colonel came back, things went back to normal.

Fortunately I had excellent driving skills. The colonel had a previously long-scheduled visit planned by his wife to visit him from America for several days. Although the Tet offensive took place just before her scheduled visit, she made the trip as planned, unaware of potential danger. The colonel and I took her to Pattaya¬ Beach, a resort on the Gulf of Thailand. Our Special Troops Unit had charge of the Army R&R center in Pattaya.

As the colonel, his wife, and I drove down a two-lane highway several days after Tet, in an Army sedan with the steering wheel on the left and driving according to the English style convention in Thailand on the left ("wrong") side of the road, I passed a long truck. All of a sudden the truck deliberately drove me off the road into the ditch at 55 mph.

I reacted instantly, hit the ditch, corrected properly, and sling shot us out of the ditch back onto the road. This masterful response allowed us all to survive. A less skillful driver could have had three dead. My white faced passengers felt very thankful. The colonel's wife cut her trip short and the next day went back to Bangkok to fly home.

At the end of my first eight-week session of taking two night college courses we had 12 days off from school before the next courses began. I had heard of a free Embassy flight the U.S. government sent around the world once a week in each direction. You needed to have the rank of a full colonel or above to fly on it. I asked my colonel if I could take a leave and go to New Delhi. He said ok and got me a flyer pass. Traveling only in civilian clothes, I arrived in New Delhi in early March 1968, one month after Tet. This completed my round the world quest by age 20. I went to the U. S. Embassy where I found restaurants by the swimming pool and 17- year-old female dependents at the Embassy's ongoing pool parties.

With Chester Bowles the U. S. Ambassador to India at the time, the 17-year-old American high school seniors invited me to go to a Ravi Shankar concert. Just a soldier from Southeast Asia who dropped in, I sat next to Mrs. Chester Bowles, the Ambassador's wife, at the concert. We had quite a night out. My colonel felt very impressed to hear about it later.

From New Delhi I flew to Kashmir where I stayed on a houseboat on Lake Srinagar, for $5.00 for one night. Art Linkletter stayed on that same houseboat just prior to my visit. Years later I sat next to him seeing the Broadway show, "42nd Street," in New York City and he confirmed staying there. Small world.

After the houseboat night I heard about a ski resort in the Himalayan Mountains and found myself taking a donkey with a group going up to Gulmarg, Kashmir, one of the most beautiful places in the world, especially in March, with views of snow on the Himalayas. I walked into the only lodge, checked in, and promptly met 20 American Peace Corps workers on holiday. In those days all male Peace Corps workers joined for only one reason, avoiding the draft. Take that, Chris Matthews. We had a lively debate about Kennedy vs McCarthy or Humphrey. I endorsed for Nixon. They couldn't believe it. They had trouble believing an active duty soldier had come there from Southeast Asia.

The next day I skied for the first time in my life. We used a rope tow. Having grown up in South Florida I never had a chance to ski. The following day we arranged for coolies with burlap tied over their feet to carry our skis up the nearby Himalayan mountain as we walked behind them, so we could ski down the pristine pathway. Not bad for my first ski experience.

With my one year of college I managed to pick up the best looking girl, a University of Michigan graduate, to travel out of there with me. We flew to New Delhi and took the train to Jaipur, the pink city. After we split I went back to New Delhi and took a train to Banaras, where they cremate bodies on the banks of the Ganges River. Next I stopped at Agra and the Taj Mahal, very beautiful. For my last stop I went to Calcutta then back to New Delhi. On this leg of the trip I realized the quality products sold in the Indian stores would sell well in America because they only cost 1/5 the price in America. I had the idea of buying products made in India and selling them in the United States two years ahead of Sam Walton, the Wal-Mart founder, but alas, I had to go back to the Army.

I walked into my Army headquarters at Camp Friendship and showed my four-day growth of beard. I had forgotten my electric shaver in the men's room of the Grand Hotel, in Calcutta. I wanted the colonel and other office staff to see me with a four-day beard before I went to the PX and bought a new shaver. The colonel, the lieutenant colonel, the sergeant major, and the beautiful 23-year-old married secretary, all felt very impressed with my travels. My colonel asked me where I planned to go next. I immediately said, "Laos."

The next session of double college night courses started that Monday night, but the next weekend I took a train to the upper Thai city across the Mekong River from Vientiane, Laos where I paid 1 Baht, $.05 for a 15-minute ride across the river in a dugout canoe. They did not have the formalities of visa and customs in this war-torn country. After eating and touring the old landmark French hotels of Vientiane I took a cab by the North Vietnam Embassy, waved to the civilians in suits standing outside, returned to the boat landing, and went back to my base in mid Thailand, all in the same day.

I did a good job for my colonel which freed him a little for working on his goal of promotion. After Tet he would spend more time with generals from Vietnam visiting Camp Friendship and let me go around checking on the progress of various projects by myself. As a 20-year-old corporal, I enjoyed going up to various first sergeants and sergeant majors checking on their project status. Once General Westmoreland and a two-star general came to visit our base. My colonel took General Westmoreland around. I took the Major General by myself for a complete tour of the base, without complaints, as I knew more about that base than anyone else.

I only regret that I didn't get to know the NCO officers in the back offices. I suspect that they had interesting stories about the Korean War. They didn't like it that a 20-year-old had so much clout and told the new replacement lieutenant colonel to try and get me transferred out. He tried and when my colonel heard about it he had this new lieutenant colonel transferred immediately to Vietnam. He lasted only about two weeks before his departure for Vietnam. So much for power during wartime.

Did I mention that no other draftee in Southeast Asia except me worked in an air-conditioned office? Only the rank of lieutenant colonel and above got this privilege. We used to go to Bangkok almost every weekend. After I dropped off the colonel I had full use of the Army sedan.

On one trip, on the outskirts of Bangkok, in a Thai taxi ahead of us going 50 mph, the rear door opened up. What looked like a pile of cardboard fell out and flopped all over the road. It did not look like a human body until it came to rest and we could identify a drunk U. S. Army lieutenant on R & R from Vietnam. I finally got to use our 1968 mobile car phone to call an ambulance. The colonel had him discharged from the Army.

After I dropped off the colonel at the Officers' Hotel I would go to the Siam Intercontinental Hotel with my Army sedan where I could meet and pick up various TWA and Pan Am around-the-world stewardesses, the best of the lot. I looked them up and visited them all over America for years afterward. Four majors on leave from Vietnam knocked on the car window when they saw me and a beautiful Southern Belle from Atlanta making out on the front seat of the Army sedan. They felt impressed.

I continued to do well for the colonel. He put me in for E-5 sergeant rank with maximum waver for time and grade, after I had one year and eight months in the Army. For my promotion to E-5 I had an oral exam with some majors covering the recent Soviet invasion of Czechoslovakia. I aced it and with the Colonels' perfect recommendation I got my promotion enabling me to go to the NCO club before my 21st birthday, where I went and had a Coke. I applied to get a 90-day early out to go back to college. I applied to USC and to Cal. Berkley without a SAT test. Both universities accepted me. The colonel offered me a recommendation for West Point. When I declined, he offered me my own Army post as commander of the Vietnam soldiers' R & R center in Pattaya Beach, if I would re-up for one year. Can you imagine a draftee commanding his own base?

I once met the granddaughter of the president of El Salvador, on her way to Spain, at the Siam Intercontinental and took her for the day to Pattaya Beach in the Army sedan on a Sunday. I wonder how many draftees can do that.

Finally, I turned down all offers for advancement in the Army, and turned 21 in Bangkok on my out-processing journey through Oakland. On the Continental Airlines flight to Hawaii I planned on a quick tour of Honolulu during the two-hour layover. After the flight landed, I ran to a waiting line of black Lincoln town cars for hire. I told the driver to drive for 20 minutes then turn around and go back so as to not miss my flight. I saw Honolulu. In three days of out- processing in Oakland, as I sat with E4 and E5 Vietnam vet sergeants on a bleacher, I waved to another full colonel who I knew from Thailand passing by. He bounded up the bleachers and wanted to know the scuttle butt on all the officers back in Camp Friendship andfor that matter all of Thailand. To have

a full colonel greet me in that way, the Vietnam vets thought I had come from Mars.

I had four years and three months left of possible reserve call-up eligibility, so I never went back to visit my old base in Malibu. I didn't want to give them any ideas. When I got out, Vietnam had another 28,000 still to die.

ENLISTED EFFICIENCY REPORT (AR 600-200 and AR 135-205)		TCO NUMBER	ROSTER NUMBER	CONTROL NUMBER

PERFORMANCE TEST SCORES OR LANGUAGE RATING SCALES (If applicable)

TEST	SCORE	TEST	SCORE	TEST	SCORE	TEST	SCORE	TEST	SCORE	TEST	SCORE

THIS SPACE FOR TCO USE

SECTION I - PERSONNEL AND ORGANIZATIONAL DATA

1. GRADE, LAST NAME, FIRST NAME, MIDDLE INITIAL, SERVICE NUMBER/SSAN, ORGANIZATION, AND ORGANIZATION ADDRESS	2. PAY GRADE E-4	3. DATE OF RANK 18 Mar 1968	4. PPD NA

SP/4 CRUEY, Ned F.
US 53 579 245
282d Engr. Det.
APO SF 96233

5. PMOS CODE 95B20	6. DATE DESIGNATED 14 Apr 1967	7. DMOS CODE 64B20

8. PURPOSE OR TYPE OF EVALUATION

[ ] MOS   [X] PROMOTION   [ ] OTHER *(Specify)*

9. MILITARY STATUS

[X] ACTIVE ARMY   [ ] RESERVE COMPONENT

10. SOURCE OF PMOS INDICATOR *(Use the code shown in the column identified by an asterisk (*) in Item 22, DA Form 20).*
(For USAEEC use)

11. a. SUPPLEMENTAL INFORMATION

11. b. [ ] RATER AND INDORSER WILL COMPLETE APPLICABLE PORTIONS OF SECTIONS III AND IV IN ADDITION TO SECTIONS II AND V.

SECTION II - RATINGS *(Read instructions on attached sheet)*

12.   RECORD YOUR RESPONSES TO THE RATING FACTORS SET FORTH HEREON FOR THE INDIVIDUAL NAMED ABOVE, DATE, AND SIGN IN THE SPACE PROVIDED.

a. RATER

RATING FACTOR						
1	[A]	[B]	[C]	[D]	[X]E	
2	[A]	[B]	[C]	[D]	[E]	[F] [X]G
3	[A]	[B]	[C]	[D]	[E]	[X]F
4	[A]	[B]	[C]	[D]	[E]	[X]F
5	[A]	[B]	[C]	[D]	[E]	[X]F
6	[A]	[B]	[C]	[D]	[E]	[F] [X]G
7	[A]	[B]	[C]	[D]	[E]	[F] [X]G
8	[A]	[B]	[C]	[D]	[E]	[X]F
9	[A]	[B]	[C]	[D]	[E]	[X]F
10	[A]	[B]	[C]	[D]	[E]	[X]F
11	[A]	[B]	[C]	[D]	[E]	[F] [X]G

b. INDORSER

[ ] MARK THIS BLOCK IF YOU DO NOT KNOW THE INDIVIDUAL BEING RATED AND CANNOT NOT COMPLETE THE INDORSEMENT.

RATING FACTOR						
1	[A]	[B]	[C]	[D]	[E]	
2	[A]	[B]	[C]	[D]	[E]	[F] [G]
3	[A]	[B]	[C]	[D]	[E]	[F]
4	[A]	[B]	[C]	[D]	[E]	[F]
5	[A]	[B]	[C]	[D]	[E]	[F]
6	[A]	[B]	[C]	[D]	[E]	[F] [G]
7	[A]	[B]	[C]	[D]	[E]	[F] [G]
8	[A]	[B]	[C]	[D]	[E]	[F]
9	[A]	[B]	[C]	[D]	[E]	[F]
10	[A]	[B]	[C]	[D]	[E]	[F]
11	[A]	[B]	[C]	[D]	[E]	[F] [G]

13. a. MONTHS COMMANDED AND/OR SUPV RATED INDIVIDUAL		13. b. GRADE OF:	
RATER	INDORSER	RATER	INDORSER

DA FORM 2166 (1 APR 68)   REPLACES DA FORM 2166, 1 APR 63, AND DA FORM 2343, 1 AUG 50, WHICH ARE OBSOLETE   PAGE 1

14. a. DUTY POSITION TITLE

Colonels Driver

b. DESCRIPTION OF DUTIES ACTUALLY PERFORMED:

15. TOE OR TD AUTHORIZED GRADE

Sgt E-5

Drive CO, Special Troops and Preform Various Office Assignments

SECTION IV - MANNER OF PERFORMANCE *(Read instructions on attached sheet)*

16. COMMENTS OF RATER

This is an outstanding, competent and highly educated soldier deserving of promotion.

17. COMMENTS OF INDORSER

SECTION V - AUTHENTICATION

DATE	TYPED NAME, GRADE, ORG AND DUTY ASG OF RATER	SIGNATURE
18. 3 Jul 61	WILLIAM J. TOWSON Colonel, Inf. Commanding	*Wm J Towson*
19. DATE	TYPED NAME, GRADE, ORG AND DUTY ASG OF INDORSER	SIGNATURE

20. THIS SOLDIER HAS BEEN PROPERLY RATED BY RATING OFFICIALS SELECTED IN ACCORDANCE WITH THE ATTACHED INSTRUCTION SHEET.

DATE	TYPED NAME, GRADE, ORG AND DUTY ASG OF REVIEWER	SIGNATURE

Note my E-5 strips, earned after 1 year and 8 months active duty.

This is the WAT that I climbed in December 1967

Chapter 14
USC Business Student with Many Lives

For my first semester at USC, starting in September 1968, I stayed with A. John Mueller, my travel companion in Europe, and I took three night courses, four credits each, at USC. I had a very boring first semester. That fall I went to an Entrepreneur Convention and bought 105 vending machines that dispensed Nabisco cookies. I had the vending machines placed at sites from Pomona to the Pacific Ocean. We constantly moved the worst selling machines to better locations. After I did a training program during September, October, and November to become a distributor for the Los Angeles Times, because of their requirement to pay $25,000.00 down for a distributorship, I took instead a newspaper distributorship for no money down with the Los Angeles Herald Examiner, owned by the Hearst family.

That Christmas John and I drove to my parents' home in Donaldson, Arkansas, half way between Arkadelphia and Malvern. They lived about 50 miles from where President Bill Clinton grew up. My parents had moved there in their early retirement during my time in the Army in Thailand to start a cattle ranch. My father had built a big apartment house in San Diego and then sold it, as his first activity as a retired man in his mid-40's. After that, my father had thought either to buy a large commercial fishing boat to take to Alaska to fish, or to buy a cattle ranch in Arkansas where you could get the most land for your money. My mother did not want the dangers associated with the commercial fishing boat so they bought the cattle ranch.

John and I left for Aspen, Colorado, the day after Christmas, with no reservations. First we went to Vail where we stayed with a couple of girls we met at the disco. We arrived in Aspen with temperatures of minus 20 degrees at night. We hung out at a cool bar/nightclub and literally asked the patrons, one by one, as they left for the night if they had a place available for us to crash. We got an invitation to a private house and the next morning woke up in a spectacular three-sided glass mansion overlooking Aspen. So much for hotel reservations. We stayed the week there then left for USC, whose football team would play in the Rose Bowl. On the way we stopped in Las Vegas for New Year's Eve, 1968 going to 1969. We stayed at the International Hotel that had just opened, and saw Gene Kelly in a musical. That hotel became the Hilton that hosted Elvis Presley as a headliner, and has now become the Westgate.

Because of my lacking social life, I pledged the top fraternity in January 1969. A pledge has to serve dinners at the fraternity house. The fraternity had a lot of parties to go to, attended by beautiful sorority girls. We averaged about two parties a week with one more casual and one more advanced, such as at somebody's parents' house. My distributorship for the Herald Examiner, an afternoon paper, which came with 12 paperboys, started February 1, 1969. This gave me plenty of money together with my GI Bill money and my 105 vending machines. That first semester in the fraternity, I lived in a nice studio apartment off campus, as it puts the pledge at risk of becoming a slave of sorts to live in the fraternity house.

That May, 1969, I sang with my fraternity together with all the fraternities and sororities at USC at the Hollywood Bowl for Songfest, a yearly tradition at that time. That summer, July 20, 1969, America landed on the moon.

To take the pressure off the next school year, I took and passed Quantitative Business Analysis (calculus) that summer. I moved into the fraternity house in the fall. Many of the members of my fraternity, children of the scions of Southern California, came from extremely wealthy and important families. Many of the girls seeking to pledge at top sororities had back up plans to go to a different university if they failed to get into the sorority that they wanted. Joining a top fraternity house gave me an immediate great social life which I welcomed. While I lived at the fraternity house, some of the younger fraternity brothers would come by at night to listen to stories of my adventures.

In 1970 and 1971 I started going to private nightclubs frequented by Hollywood movie stars in Beverly Hills. How to crack this crowd? I paid for a membership in The Factory, a declining private club where I met several entertainment lawyers whom I befriended. Through their client contacts they got me into some of the more exclusive clubs, including The Candy Store and The Daisy on a regular basis.

The last and hardest to access of the private clubs, Bumbles, on Robertson, created the greatest challenge. I went with my friend John and we tried unsuccessfully to get in. Before we left we went around back and while looking in the kitchen window John recognized a kitchen worker who use to work at his father's five star restaurant on Balboa Island. The kitchen worker let us in through the kitchen.

That event changed my life. I felt determined to meet someone inside who could get me in for the future. I did, a young starlet, and from then on I could go to Bumbles. I met one girl who said her father had high ranking in the Mafia. To prove it she asked me if I would like to meet Frank Sinatra, a friend of the family. I declined. I started to bring fraternity brothers to these clubs to mix up the social scene.

One night I brought a frat member to Bumbles who joined the fraternity before me. He recognized a fellow frat member who had already graduated from USC. As we talked, he said he liked working as a stockbroker for Merrill Lynch. It dawned on me that I should become a stockbroker with my imminent Bachelor of Science degree in Business Administration, with a major in finance, marketing, and management. As a first problem, a stock broker on the West Coast has to get up at 5:00 am. I did not want to get up early the rest of my life the way I did when I had the paper routes as a teenager. It dawned on me to move to New York City, an idea planted in my mind from my 21-year-old model girlfriend who I met in Acapulco six years earlier.

The previous summer I got a California real estate license, but with interest rates for home loans at 21%, nothing could sell. Management offered me commercial real estate after I graduated but I had my mind set on New York City. I owned 105 Nabisco vending machines which didn't make much money. My friend Steve, who I met in 1966 on the ship between New York and Southampton after finishing a stint in the Coast Guard to avoid the draft during the Viet Nam War, died in a diving accident, ending my plan for a California conglomerate. IBM offered me a position as a management trainee just from coming around and servicing one of my vending machines at their Wilshire Boulevard office. Naturally I talked to the managers when I visited.

USC played in the Rose Bowl all three years I attended. We had to come back six days early from skiing in Aspen to go to the Rose Bowl. What a hardship! Hollywood came calling by way of inviting our fraternity members to go on some of the television shows as extras. I found it boring and left after half a day.

The Delta Gamma (Dee Gees) sorority invited me to attend several dinners at their sorority house resulting in my getting elected as their Anchorman in 1970. Later I took a Delta Gamma sorority girlfriend in my new convertible sports car for a 10-day ski trip during Spring Break, previously unheard of at conservative USC for sorority girls to travel with boys. We went to Las Vegas, Jackson Hole, Sun Valley, and San Francisco.

In Las Vegas we watched gamblers once again at the International Hotel and Casino. When my girlfriend flirted with black jack players who proceeded to loose extra amounts of money, the casino comped us free tickets to Little Richard's midnight show.

Two months later at age 23, I left the USC graduation ceremony, picked up my already-packed suitcase from my fraternity house residence, and started driving to my next home, New York City.

USC Graduate Photo

Just graduated college June 1971 in Donaldson AR on my way to NYC with my college car.

When I got in through the kitchen at Bumbles,
this is who I met to get me future access.
Danell Steele

Chapter 15
Getting Started in New York, New York

After traveling around the country for 3 weeks I arrived in Manhattan on June 30, 1971. I spent the first night sleeping in my 1970 Pontiac LeMans Super Sport Convertible under the Brooklyn Bridge. I had no debt but very little cash left. As a 23-year-old I had a resume that would choke the proverbial horse. I literally lived on my American Express Card until I got my first job on August 12th.

The second day in town I looked up an old girlfriend who I had not seen in five years, whose father owned Abraham Chevrolet in South Florida. She got me connected with a roommate situation in Hell's Kitchen, for $50 per month. That fall I used The Village Voice to get a great apartment sharing option, in the Midtown East area.

It took a month to get in a stockbroker training program on Wall Street for Shields and Company, 44 Wall Street, starting August 12, the day President Nixon took the United States off of the Gold Standard. I became the youngest in my class of investment banker trainees at the age of 23, two years younger than the standard age for beginning this training since I had such an extensive resume. The Series Seven training took a year.

The Xerox management training group in Fort Lauderdale and the IBM management training group in Los Angeles had both offered me positions, as had Viacom in New York, but I wanted the stock market. I even considered a position in the compliance department of the New York Stock Exchange. After training, I used the reverse phonebook directory to call potential customers. I called everyone on Fifth Avenue, Park Avenue, Central Park South, Central Park West, as well as Sutton Place, and Beekman Place.

I saw a chance to network socially and by Christmas I became an informal party broker. In 1971, I went to 23 Christmas parties although I knew no one in town six months earlier. I heard of Seven Sisters College mixers taking place around Manhattan. When I called Information, they had different schools like Smith, Wellesley, and Vassar listed. I found out the dates of the mixers and showed up.

I met my first wife, a third year medical student and the most attractive girl in her class, at a Smith, Wellesley, and Vassar mixer at the New York Yacht Club. The sorority girls or Hollywood starlets I had known in LA certainly never had an advanced degree let alone a medical degree. When I showed up with her socially at the med school events, her fellow students wanted to see if they could show me up, but in a friendly way. I more than held my own even winning in Scrabble among doctors. They tried to defeat me, but to no avail.

As a stockbroker trainee I had to sit at the desks of older brokers who went on vacation. I had a problem in having no experience in finishing the business day at 5 pm. I could spend a small fortune between 5 pm and midnight. I needed extra work to occupy my time. While substituting, I overheard another broker saying that when it got slow in the brokerage business for a broker friend of his, his friend had obtained a taxi license. With that idea I secretly got a taxi license but I didn't use it until I completed my training four months later. After my training I transferred to midtown to the Columbia Pictures Building at 55th St on 5th Ave, which became the Coca Cola Building later.

I could drive a cab in the evening and always make money instead of spending money. I visited the VA and asked what benefits they had for Vets. They said I could buy a house or a taxicab. I soon bought a cab, Medallion Number 6N86, and all of a sudden I started making real money again.

In 1973, I paid $16,000.00 for my original taxi medallion. Two months before I bought it, you could buy two medallions for $25,000.00. The price continued to go up by over $1,000.00 per month for many years. Eventually, the price of a single medallion went up to more than $1,000,000.00.

A taxi medallion in New York City gives the owner the right to have a taxicab with that designated number and to pick up fares in New York City, 24 hours a day; seven days a week. All of a sudden I could make money every hour of my life.

The first month of owning a cab in 1973, a war started in Israel. America had its first experience with cars waiting in line to buy gas. When I waited to get gas, besides filling up the gas tank of the cab I also filled up the five, five-gallon gas cans that I carried with me. That allowed me to save a future wait of several hours. I had to keep 25 gallons of fuel on the fire escape at my apartment on 50th Street between 1st and 2nd Avenues. I wonder if I broke any fire laws.

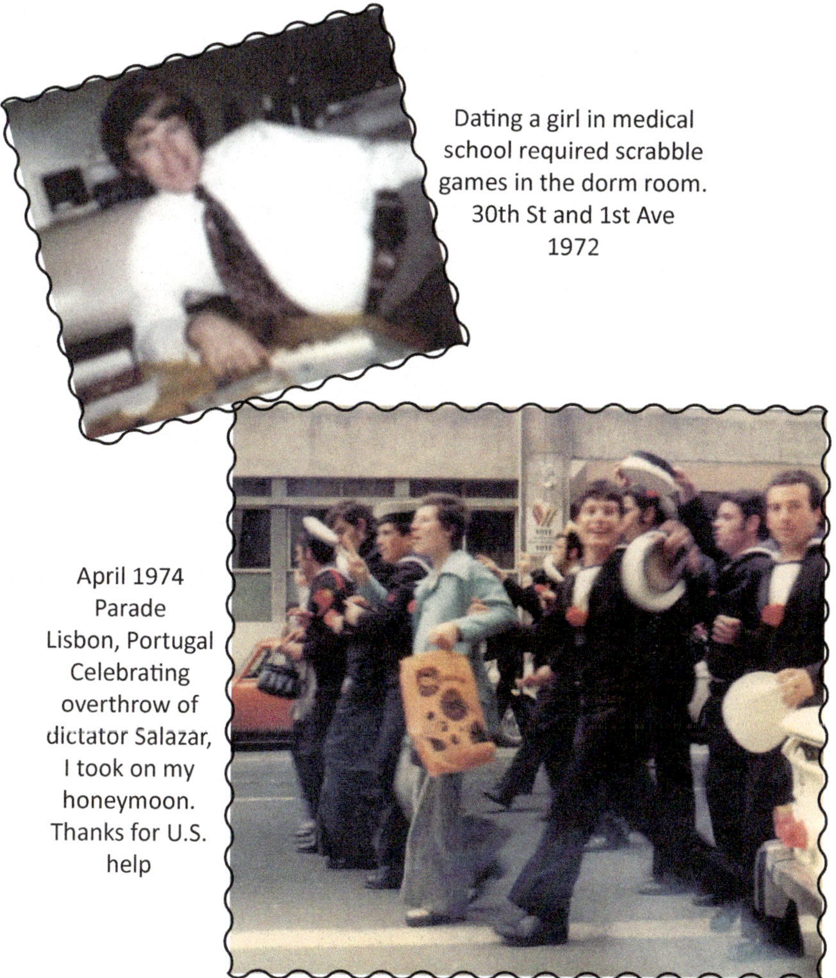

Dating a girl in medical school required scrabble games in the dorm room. 30th St and 1st Ave 1972

April 1974
Parade
Lisbon, Portugal
Celebrating
overthrow of
dictator Salazar,
I took on my
honeymoon.
Thanks for U.S.
help

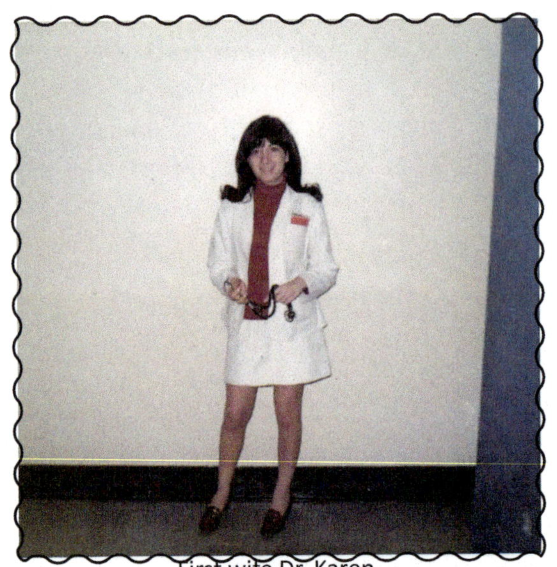

First wife Dr. Karen.
A graduate of Wellesley, same class as
Hillary, and NYU Medical Schoool

On the wind jammer
Harvey Gamage in the
summer of 1974, when
the group of military
helicopters flew over the
ship in their way to pick up
Nelson Rockefeller at his
summer home in Maine.
We deduced that Gerald
Ford had picked him for
Vice President.

Our rental
car in the
soviet state of
Georgia, USSR,
1975

Machu
Picchu
1976

Chapter 16
World Travel as a Couple

After I married my pediatrician girlfriend at age 26, we traveled the world for one month a year on her intern and resident program vacations. We lived in hospital housing on 69th Street between First and York.

We took a one-week windjammer cruise, the Harvey Gamage, on vacation in Maine. We drove to the dock in my taxi. We saw several Air Force helicopters flying up the coast of Maine in mid-August 1974 to the home of Nelson Rockefeller. We knew that the presence of those helicopters there meant that President Gerald Ford had picked Nelson Rockefeller for his vice president.

We visited Portugal in April 1974, arriving on the same day they overturned their dictatorship of 50 years. I marched in their parade. People thanked me, thinking of me as part of the CIA who may have helped them get their freedom. We went on to tour Spain and Morocco.

The next June, 1975, we flew to Norway where we looked up my old French Riviera girlfriend. She had become a dentist and had a baby. We drove to Stockholm and took a ferry to Helsinki where we caught a prearranged train to visit the Soviet Union for a month, deluxe class. At the first stop, St. Petersburg, we observed the police state first hand. In Moscow, we stayed at the National Hotel for two or three days, right off of Red Square, the same hotel where Lenin stayed when he came to take over the country in 1917. The hotel had a band that played from 8:30 to 10:30 pm. At the National Hotel, they threw a small cocktail party for us, a 27-year-old pediatrician and a 27-year-old businessman from America, and had 30 top University of Moscow students meet with us at the cocktail party. I suspect that V. Putin may well have come with the group. We imagined that Moscow had had few deluxe class tourists of our age. Moscow had a daily English-language newspaper apparently printed by Pravda, the Russian state news organization. To find a newspaper with more balanced news, one day I went to the U. S. Embassy in Moscow where they allowed me to read the international newspaper, The Herald Tribune, in the lobby.

On a train ride in Russia, we met a married couple, both engineers, and in their late 20's like us. They saw a copy of the National Geographic magazine that I had with me. They felt eager to look at the advertisements in the magazine, something they had never seen. We calculated out the relative income levels for our particular situations versus their junior engineer salaries, which came out to 66:1.

We flew down to the Soviet province of Georgia where we rented a car to drive to Sochi, on the black sea by way of Gori, Stalin's home town. None of the roads had proper signs ever since the Nazi invasion. We came to a fork in the road, stopped the car, got out, and saw two Soviet Air Force pilots walking along the road. We asked them for directions to Gori. They said they would show us, because they needed a ride. We went only a mile down the road until the police pulled us over and arrested our uniformed passengers. They escorted us to the Intourist office in the next town where they said don't pick up any riders, and then they let us go.

On an overnight train in the Ukraine I locked the bathroom door to wash my hair in the sink. The police nearly broke the door down when I did not open it immediately after they started knocking.

Even though we traveled deluxe class, half the time the hotel had no hot water. Every meal took two hours of waiting to get the one available dish, chicken Kiev, but we had a great adventure. In Odessa our guide spoke perfect English so we asked her story. We felt incredulous when we learned that her parents re-immigrated back to the Soviet Union from her home in Detroit. She said her father had deteriorating vision and they got more medical care in the Ukraine than in Detroit. I regret that we brought her to tears to tell her the benefits that she missed by leaving the United States.

The following January we flew to Belize and toured every country except Chile in Central and South America for one month.

We visited the Mayan ruins of Tikal in Guatemala and visited the

Panama Canal. While taking a train down the mountain from Quito to Guayaquil, Ecuador, they stopped the train and backed it up because of a threat by bandits or rebels on the train tracks. They put us on a bus, and we had a very dangerous ride down the narrow, winding road out of the Andes.

In Peru, we visited Lima, Lake Titicaca, Cusco, and Machu Picchu. At the corner of Argentina, Paraguay, and Brazil, we went to the huge Iguassu Falls. We visited Buenos Aires one month before Isabella Peron got deposed, with the currency experiencing a meltdown. We bought a lot of beautiful leather goods at bargain prices. When we ate at the best restaurant at the Hilton Hotel in Buenos Aires, a full-course meal cost under $1.00 per person in U.S. currency. We saw people arriving without suitcases and buying all the leather goods possible.

I acknowledge that some men do not mature as fast as women. After my wife took the pediatric boards four months later on May 15, 1976, I told her that I wanted a trial separation, the hardest thing I ever did. At age 28, I wanted to become a bachelor again. I wanted a more exciting life.

Chapter 17
Traveling the Pacific Rim as a Single Man

After I became single on May 15, 1976, the next month I completed the arrangements for my next big trip. I turned in my expensive taxi license plates. I moved out of my hotel at 28th and Madison where I lived for only a month. Saving on commercial taxi insurance and rent payments helped pay for my upcoming three-month tour of the Pacific Rim countries. Looking back on those times, I made the right decision in pulling out of the stock market as a broker, as the stock market stayed flat until 1982. We also had a recession going on, that I did not learn about until I read about it many years later. We each have only one short life, so make good decisions.

As my first stop, I went to North Dakota where I briefly studied the possibility of large scale wheat farming as a great future business. The previous winter I met a wheat farmer from the Dakotas while traveling in Peru. He convinced me of the ultimate future growth potential of wheat farming. From Vancouver, British Columbia, I took a cruise ship to Alaska and enjoyed spending time with the younger people on board. At the end of the cruise in Alaska, I flew to Point Barrow and Prudhoe Bay, an oil company town in the process of starting up Alaska oil production. I walked on the frozen Arctic Ocean in June 1976. I flew to Fairbanks, from which I had a cab drop me just out of town so I could hitchhike to Anchorage.

As I stood on the two-lane road on the edge of town, waiting for a ride, surrounded by woods about 8:00 am, two drunk Indians came walking along the road. As they started to circle me, I started to run, with my cash for the trip and my airline tickets in my shoulder bag, my only luggage. Just then the once-a-day Greyhound Bus came by. I went out in the middle of the road and stopped the bus. I got on, paid, and took a seat for the eight-hour ride next to a cute 25 year old nun. By the end of the ride I think she might have considered rejoining the secular world, but her brother and his entire family came to the bus station to pick her up.

From Anchorage I made my way to Taiwan, Okinawa, and then to Japan. I took a bullet train to Kyoto where I spent time with an attractive British girl. She traveled with me in Japan including Hiroshima until I went on to Korea. I toured the Philippines and then Hong Kong, from where I took the water shuttle to Macao. I walked around Macao, and then took the water shuttle back to Hong Kong. The day I arrived in Hong Kong, Jimmy Carter picked Walter Mondale to become his vice presidential running mate. When I went to Thailand and revisited my old Army base, the former Camp Friendship, which the U. S. had given to the Thai Army, I managed to bluff my way on base to see it.

From the north of Thailand, I went into Burma, including Rangoon, the capital city, and took an overnight trip to Pagan, the home of 1,000 pagodas, where I got escorted around in an Army Willys Jeep leftover from World War II and made in Toledo, Ohio, the city of my birth. From there I went on to Bangladesh, proceeded to Calcutta, and took a train to Darjeeling, the tea capital of India, in the foothills of the Himalayas.

When coming back through the mountains from Darjeeling by cab we encountered two large trucks that had collided and backed up the traffic on the mountain road. I simply paid my driver, walked to the other end of the traffic jam, and hired the last vehicle stuck to turn around and take me to Calcutta.

From Calcutta in India, I flew to Katmandu, Nepal, to the Himalayan foothills. After that, I went down to New Delhi and caught a flight to Bangalore. In Bangalore I went to the front of the taxi line and offered the driver $50 a day to travel straight south to the tip of India and up the western coast all the way to Bombay. It took about four days. They had a lot of one-lane roads and no rental car agencies. When another car came along, you would just pull over. Very few Westerners visited this exotic part of the real India. I would stay in hotels and the driver would sleep in the car, excited to make $50 a day. After touring Bombay, I said goodbye to the cab driver in Bombay.

I flew from Bombay to Madras and then flew to Kuala Lumpur, where

I had a cab driver who drove very fast, just racing from the airport to downtown. When I asked him to slow down he turned around and said "Shut up or I will kill you". I shut up. I could have used the Uber rating system then.

I flew to Singapore, then Jakarta, and on to Bali where I took a slow, boring sailboat ride where I asked them to pull near the shore. I got into the water, swam to shore, and walked back to my hotel. Because of the slow pace, I never did like sailing very much.

From the continuously hot and humid weather, I had some heat rash which disappeared upon arrival in Sydney in early August 1976, in the dead of winter. I took off for Thredbo, a ski resort, in the mountains outside of the capital, Canberra, Australia. As I traveled light, I put on everything in my bag on for warmth and skied all day.

I went on to tour Melbourne, on to Adelaide, the Great Outback and up to Ayers Rock (also known as Uluru).

In a rented Avis Ford Cortina with small wheels, driving 80 mph on the last paved road before hitting 1,000 miles of dirt road, just outside of Port Augusta in lower central Australia, out of nowhere a 250 pound Emu ran in front of my vehicle. Australia had no fences in that part of the continent. I jammed on the brakes probably down to 60 mph, but the car simply planed sideways. After missing the Emu, the vehicle flipped over about six times on the side of the dirt road. I had just gassed up so I wanted to get out fast. I had to crawl out of the broken windshield with the vehicle turned upside down. Other cars stopped. Someone called an ambulance from nearby Port Augusta. I tried to get up and for the first and only time in my life I couldn't get up or move my legs. For one hour I wondered if I would ever move again. The ambulance came, built a lift under me and transported me to the nearest hospital.

Medical staff did two things first, take my blood test for alcohol and at my urgent request obtained an x-ray to see if I had broken my back. I laid there, waiting for the results that would determine the rest of my life. They came and told me I had nothing broken just several traumatized back muscles, and I would recover. Would you like the free wing of the hospital with the aborigines or the cost-money section with the Whites? I took the free wing of the hospital where I shared a room with two aboriginal men. I had my biggest accomplishment my first night in the hospital by rolling over once without passing out from the muscle pain.

After the second night in the hospital I called Avis to pick me up with another car. I paid the $250 deductible fee for totaling the car, got in the car slowly, and continued on to the Great Outback and my epic trip. Just before I got to the desert the last hotel had no rooms available. I had to drive through the night at 30 degree temperatures with severe back pain from muscle spasms that got worse with cold. I would stop the car every so often and sleep until it got cold enough to trigger the muscle spasms in my back, which woke me up. It still ranks as my worst night ever.

I had breakfast in Coober Pedy, the opal capital of the world, then continued on to Ayers Rock where I couldn't walk one foot up the rock. I drove the four and a half hours to Alice Springs where somehow I met some local girls and found myself in a romantic situation with a very sore back. I dropped off my rental car and flew to Darwin where my female cab driver had the last name, Darwin, interesting and romantic. I flew to Cairns where more painful romance occurred at this Australian resort off the Great Barrier Reef. I felt so tempted to scuba dive the reef, but the cold water in the dead of winter and the pain in my back convinced me not to go diving.

I flew to New Guinea, where I toured Port Moresby, the capital city of New Guinea and a major ally in World War II in defeating the Japanese. I flew to Mount Hagen in the interior where I saw naked young native woman with painted faces, wearing beads and unusual hairdos shopping in a C store. In Mount Hagen I also met some American female teachers on vacation in New Guinea, teaching for a year in Brisbane, Australia. They invited me to stay at their rented house when I passed through on my way down the coast back to Sydney. Arriving back in Cairns while waiting customs it finally hit me that I needed to have a bowel movement for the first time since the car accident eleven days before. I ran to the bathroom and left my passport with the customs agent. When I got back I found out he had accidentally given my passport to an American family who followed me through customs. They rented a car and took off for Sydney. We had no way to reach them until they turned their car in to Avis in Sydney, so I drove to Sydney with no passport.

I visited the young teachers in Brisbane who I had met in New

Guinea, where the most memorable event took place when they discovered a tarantula and instead of stomping on it, they maced it. Mace causes the nearby people to cough. Coughing can cause extreme pain to someone with severe pulled back muscles still healing. Because of the painful coughing, I left at 4:00 am, drove to Sydney, picked up my passport at Avis, and soon flew to Fiji.

Fiji has warm water and the clearest ocean in the world. I barely felt ready to scuba dive but had my first open ocean dive ever since my certification in a New Jersey quarry two months before. On my first open ocean dive, I went 120 feet down, still my deepest and clearest dive ever. I dove an amazing 1890 shipwreck. I had no back pain in the water, only getting in and out.

From Fiji I flew to the north island of New Zealand, arriving on a Sunday. I had my first experience in a country that completely shuts down on Sunday. I felt lucky to get a toasted cheese sandwich in the hotel coffee shop. While walking around town that evening someone invited me to go to Sunday night church services, which I enjoyed. Subsequently, I heard that New Zealand made the Sunday closings more liberal.

The next day, Monday, I rented a car and started touring the north island. I ferried over to the south island where in a hotel I met a very pretty and very aristocratic English tourist who spoke the Queen's English. We traveled around the south island and at the end took a ski plane up to Mt. Cook that circled around the mountains, the most beautiful scenery I had ever seen from an airplane. The plane landed on skis, and skied to a stop. We walked around the stunning top of Mt. Cook, before boarding the plane again, which skied back into its takeoff, the most scenic flight ever.

From New Zealand I went on to Tahiti, the main island of the Society Islands of French Polynesia, including the islands of Tahiti, Moorea, and Bora Bora. During my four days at Club Med in Moorea, the flagship facility, I did everything they offered and left three days early. I wanted to make the most of my time. Canadian Prime Minister Pierre Trudeau met his future wife, Margaret, at that Club Med. I had great fun, and then went on to Bora Bora.

Bora Bora ranks with the Himalayas for the most beautiful places in the world, a place for lots of romance and snorkeling. I heard that 5,000

U.S. Army soldiers spent three years waiting for a Japanese invasion that didn't come. They built the roads. I still had better Army duty in Thailand, but Bora Bora came in second.

For my next stop I met my friend John in Hawaii, where we visited all the islands. We saw Don Ho perform. In early September 1976 in Hawaii, more romance happened and Mao Tse Tung died.

Note to future billionaires — work hard, save your money, and in your sixties or seventies go on the Pacific Rim trip I have just described: not!

When I went back to L.A. from Hawaii, I briefly resumed dating my sorority girl friend from 1971 for two or three days. I went on to Las Vegas where I saw Linda Ronstadt in concert then flew back to resume my life in New York City.

Prudoe Bay
Alaska
1976
On Grand tour
of the Pacific
Rim

On the Arctic
Ocean off Pt
Barrow
Alaska
1976

With my English
girlfriend, who spoke
the Queen's English, on
Mt. Cook, New Zealand,
after the most beautiful
plane ride in the world
on my Pacific Rim trip
of 1976

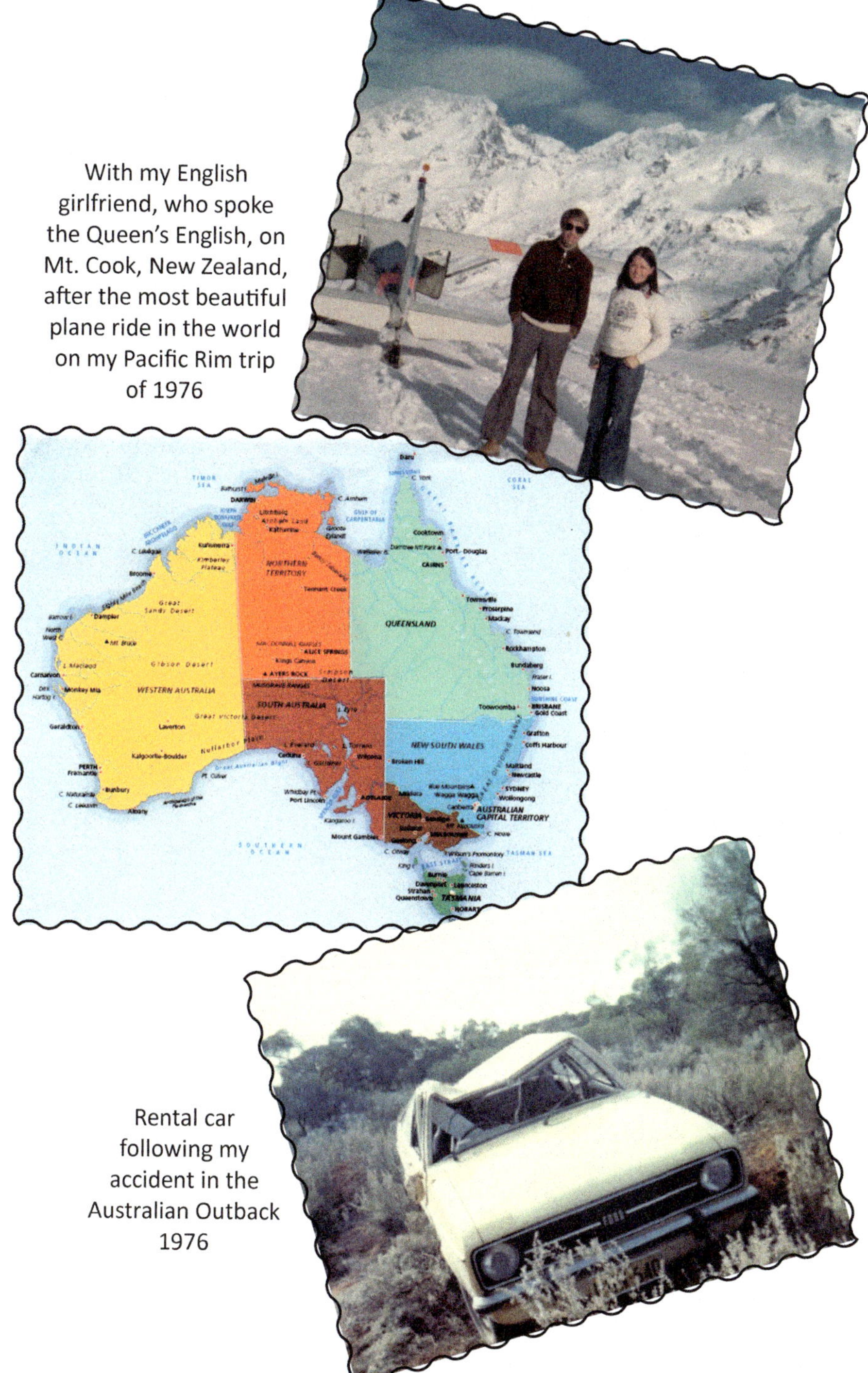

Rental car
following my
accident in the
Australian Outback
1976

Photo Caption for Philippines 1976

In 1976 on a raft trip as a tourist in the Philippines as part of my Pacific Rim trip. With the country under martial law with the requirement to get off the streets by 12 midnight or make oneself subject to getting shot by the police under the presidency of Ferdinand Marcus, one night I almost did not make it back to my hotel by midnight

Chapter 18
The First of Six Years in Greenwich Village

With no residence I picked up my paid off Checker Cab and medallion with all my worldly possessions in the trunk, at the end of September 1976.

I picked up my new license plates and started working to make some money. That afternoon I drove to a taxi stand at 9th Street and 6th Ave in Greenwich Village, parked, and started looking for a close by studio apartment. I found a recent vacancy at 68 W 10th Street, one short block away. A previous occupant had just died. I secured the $175 a month rent controlled lease for only a $400 cash bribe to the superintendent. He needed one month to fix the studio up so he let me crash for the month of October in the basement on a cot with my sleeping bag in the building's paint and supply room. After a month, I took possession and made my first home as a single man age 29, custom and very comfortable to my taste. When in Singapore, I had picked up 400 cassette tapes of all music to date at a pirate music shop. I often would drive my cab from 8:00 am to 11:45 pm at times seven days a week. Everything went for one last grand trip in the summer of 1977 and a future taxi fleet.

In March, 1977, someone crashed into the back of my Checker taxi, while it was parked at my local cab stand. Naturally the police came and took my trunk possessions of 400 CD's, a heavy, luxury suede winter coat that I had bought in Buenos Aires the year before, and $600 in cash. I had to buy another Checker taxi.

Chapter 19
Adventures in Africa, Afghanistan, and Elsewhere

In June of 1977 I left the Manhattan docks on the ocean liner Queen Elizabeth II travelling to Southampton, England, the beginning of another three to four month trip. Coming into the Southampton Harbor, a 50-mile channel, for the Queen's Silver Jubilee Celebration the entire British Navy welcomed us with 21-gun salutes all along the 50-mile channel. What a treat!

I hung out with Betty Friedan and her medical student daughter on the ship. I met two English girls on the ship who I invited to tour with me in France and into Spain. I rented a car in France. We drove down through Biarritz and on to Pamplona where they have the running of the bulls.

From Pamplona I went to Madrid, and eventually flew to Marbella on the Spanish Riviera. On this delayed flight, I hung out with and talked extensively with my seat mate, actor Ray Milland. I enjoyed mingling with Swedish tourists in Marbella, a fancy night club resort. From there I flew to Algiers, Algeria, and on to Niamey, Niger the only world capital with all dirt roads.

In Niamey, Niger, I applied to go on the bus ride to Gao, Mali. They told me that because of canceling last week's bus, the current bus had gotten fully loaded, but I could still go in crowded conditions. The bus had a wooden bench on each side and a double wooden bench in the middle. Everybody had their legs interlaced with the legs of the people in front of them and people even sat on top of the backrest of the center wooden benches. The bus had a significant level of overcrowding. I had sardine cans and bottled water, in July on the perimeter of the Sahara. At 1:00 am the bus stopped in the middle of the desert on our dirt road and the driver announced that we would sleep there. We all got off the bus and lay down on the desert floor. I remember laying down on the African dirt with my backpack for my pillow, looking up at the stars, and thinking "Best night ever."

The next day while crossing the Niger-Mali border I saw a Land Rover with three Doctors without Borders, doctors traveling north. I talked my way into a ride with them and got off the bus. As we drove along the Niger River in the heat of the day I talked them into going for a swim to cool off. We went. I had to go to the bottom of the four-foot deep river to get to the cool water.

Arriving in Gao, the only hotel in town gave me a bucket of water for my room when I checked in. No air conditioning. Four times that night I got up and poured water on myself so I could go back to sleep. It worked. The next morning I dunked my jeans into the bucket and put them on and took off walking around town. I met a Baptist missionary and as we walked back to his house for lemonade I suddenly found myself unable to speak. The Sahara desert heat dried up my voice cords and my jeans in 30 minutes. That afternoon I went to the airport for the once-a-week flight to Timbuktu. Thirty other people also wanted to go stand by. They came into the airport and announced they had only one pull down seat left on the otherwise full plane. We all wanted it. I vaulted over the counter, jammed a $50 bill into the agent's hand and said, "Let's go. " We went. The others handed me mail to deliver. No problem. After Timbuktu I went on to Bamako and then along the coast to the many West African countries, finally arriving in Lagos, Nigeria. Lagos had two interesting things. No available hotel space. After several hours of the top hotel switchboard operator trying to find me a room to no avail, I simply walked down the long hallway and laid down on the carpet behind a desk and went to sleep. In the middle of the night another tourist walked down the same hall and laid down near me. They had no rooms. In Lagos you could trade $100 US bills into $200 Nigeria money on the black market. This helped for one reason. Because the airlines buy Nigerian oil they had to honor Nigerian money at face value for airline tickets. I bought all the rest of my airline tickets for ½ price. What a deal.

The next morning I got a Portuguese flight going from Lagos, Nigeria, non-stop to Johannesburg, South Africa. The flight had one glitch. For unclear reasons, the Belgian airliner made an unauthorized 15-minute stop in Salisbury, Rhodesia, an outlaw country with world sanctions and under civil war, with the insurgents led by Mugabe, who later became president of Zimbabwe. Well, I really wanted to go to Rhodesia but couldn't find an airline to go there so I simply took my shoulder bag, walked off the plane, and went through customs by myself. The airline personnel freaked out because it constituted a break with some kind of international air law to leave a flight, in such a way. They sent a crew to hunt me down and force me back on the plane.

I ran to the parking lot and crawled under a car where I waited one hour for the personnel from the large plane finally to give up and leave. After the plane left, the Rhodesians at the airport welcomed me. They asked me if I came as a mercenary. I said no, just a tourist, and as it turned out, the only tourist. They felt proud to show their beleaguered countrymen that they still had a tourist industry and put me on national TV. I went to the casino downtown by the hotel in Salisbury, and played roulette for a few rolls. The next day, I got a free, military escorted jeep ride to Karamu Lake and Victoria Falls, then Salisbury with a machine-gun mounted jeep in front of and behind my vehicle.

From Salisbury, Rhodesia, I flew to Johannesburg in the morning. I took a cab to the train station and asked, do you go to Kimberley and Cape Town. Unbeknownst to me the once- a-week Blue Train would leave in 15 minutes for Cape Town. The Blue Train, one of the world's most exotic train rides scheduled by tourists and sold out many months or even years in advance, had space available in the caboose held open for Blacks to ride at the last minute. The caboose had no other riders. I had the caboose to myself as my personal train car for this two-day trip. We stopped in Kimberly, a gold mining town, in the middle of the night, which I saw looking out the window.

In Cape Town when I rented a car they told me they had a fuel shortage because of world anti-apartheid sanctions and sometimes they had all gas stations closed. I toured all over South Africa including Kruger National Park to see the wild animals. Driving from Kruger back to Jo Berg – colloquial for Johannesburg – since they stopped selling gas at noon on Friday, they had no open gas stations, so I ran out of gas about 80 miles short of Jo Berg in the middle of nowhere. I simply pulled over, locked the car and started hitchhiking. I got a ride with a local Black family and offered them $20 to take me to the Intercontinental Hotel in Jo Berg. The car had half the floor board missing on a cold winter night, but I felt happy. The next day I walked into Avis and told them where to pick up their vehicle. They said, it happens all the time. On my way to the airport I had the taxi driver take me on a tour of Soweto, a Black township in the suburbs of Johannesburg, home of many, ongoing anti-Apartheid demonstrations.

For my next stop I flew into Nairobi, Kenya, and rented a car. I drove through Massai territory where they chased me for taking their picture. I got away. Who knew? I went to the Masa Mara game preserve and stayed at a lodge. They told me to take great care, which I did, going to my room after dinner because sometimes the lions come down to drink from the swimming pool at night. The next morning I got up early to drive to a special lake to see the crocodiles and hippos. I actually felt in danger and only stayed a short while as I had gone alone. From my rental car, I saw lions, giraffes, and elephants everywhere, even on the dirt road with me. I even herded wildebeest with my car by splitting their convoy. I got up another morning and went about one hundred miles out of my way to Olduvai Gorge with no one else there, where Dr. Leakey discovered three to four million year old human ancestors. As I drove to the coast to go scuba diving I saw a very cute early 20's Australian female hitchhiking on her way to Tanzania then to South Africa for a sailboat trip to South America. She had just spent a year hitching through Asia and another year in Europe. What nerve she had, and what risk she took! Even I do not recommend this, and I take a lot of chances.

After getting back to the Nairobi Airport and turning in my car I found they had a once-a-week flight to Uganda which still had Idi Amin as the dictator. I said, why not, and found myself the lone passenger on the once a week flight. Arriving at the Entebbe Airport I thought it safest to stay at the airport hotel. They gave me a bottle of orange soda when I checked in. It turns out the room had no running water. I brushed my teeth with orange soda with ants all over the floor, the second on my all-time list of exotic nights. I took several cabs around the capital and by Lake Victoria. People would spot me, run up to me, and say to me, "Tell the world, they are killing us all." It really happened. I left on the next flight out.

I flew into Addis Ababa, Ethiopia, and the comfort of the Hilton Hotel, a country under total Communist dictatorship at the time. Everywhere I looked I saw pictures of Marx, Engels, Lenin, and Brezhnev.

The next day I flew to the Sudan where the White Nile and the Blue Nile meet. In Khartoum, I went to an outdoor ancient museum with artifacts from the Nubian civilization 3,000 or 4,000 years before, when Sudan briefly ruled the world. At that time the Sahara Desert hardly existed.

From the Sudan at the end of July 1977, I flew to Peshawar, Pakistan while stopping in Jeddah, Saudi, Arabia, and Dubai. It had temperatures almost equivalent to those in the Sahara Desert.

In Peshawar I took a bus down the winding road through the Khyber Pass into Afghanistan, a sleepy country, on into Kabul. King Dowd still remained in power at the time, one or two years before the Russians invaded, with the 30-year war about to begin. I only regret not traveling around more in Afghanistan. After Ronald Reagan assumed the U. S. Presidency, starting in 1981 he had hand-held Stinger missiles given to every Afghani man that wanted one. A Stinger missile could bring down a helicopter or airplane. The Russians soon pulled out in defeat and the Taliban entered.

In addition to the issues in Afghanistan, the USSR collapsed about ten years later, with associated other disasters including the Chernobyl nuclear meltdown and the earthquakes in the southern Soviet states where the shoddy workmanship in apartment buildings led to the deaths of untold thousands of people.

As a Vietnam-era veteran, I like to think that through the Viet Nam war we contributed to depleting the Soviet Union financially, and to the eventual collapse of the Soviet Union, since they backed the North Vietnamese and the Viet Cong. Take credit, my fellow Vietnam era veterans. You will not read this anywhere else. Take credit.

From Afghanistan, I went to Tehran, Iran, where I rented a car and drove to Shiraz, Isfahan, and Quom. I visited Persepolis an ancient capital of the Persian Empire. The food in the countryside tasted so awful to me that I ate only watermelon for two days. With the Shah still in power, I could fly directly into Israel.

In Israel I rented another car and while driving through the Golan Heights I picked up four, hitch hiking soldiers with machine guns. I felt very secure. Although I had visited Jerusalem in Jordan before the 1967 war, I had never before gone to Israel. After going to all the usual tourist stops I drove down through the Sinai Desert to the resort town of Mueba to go scuba diving. I got stuck in some desert sand while trying to find a supposed European nudist colony and had to have a tractor pull me out. I loved the scuba diving.

From Israel I went to Rome and then to Nice in the French Riviera, my favorite playground as a 29 year old. I met one 21-year-old girl while dancing in Monaco who had her own chauffeured stretch Rolls Royce. What a fun ride! The next morning we woke up to the news that Elvis had died, and to find the chauffeur still waiting in the Rolls.

In St. Tropez and Monaco, I used to go up to docked yachts having early evening cocktail parties, introduce myself as staying at the Hotel de Paris, and ask to attend the party. They always invited me.

Treetops Hotel, Kenya 1977, where Princess Elizabeth learned her father had died in 1952.

Herding giraffes with my rental car in Kenya 1977

Chapter 20
My Taxi Fleet and
More Manhattan Bachelor Stories

When I got back to New York City, I knew I needed to start a taxi fleet, if for no other reason than to improve my social position. Now I know I should have bought Manhattan real estate instead, like Donald Trump.

In the late fall of 1977 I traded in the equity of my paid-off taxi medallion and purchased four medallions. I bought two more medallions in January 1978 and two more in March, with my own equity plus down payments. Soon I could see clearly that this business would become profitable soon and that it would need lots of capital to operate.

That February 1978 I still found time to go skiing in several top resorts in the Alps for two weeks and to spend two weeks in the Caribbean scuba diving. In August, 1978, I found time to go skiing in Portillo, Chile. While sitting around the lodge, the subject of Studio 54 – a famous, exclusive night club on 54th Street and Eighth Avenue in New York City -- came up. I told the group that that I went to Studio 54 on a regular basis. One guy canceled his travel plans so he could fly back to New York with me and go to Studio 54. I got him a date and we went on a double date to Studio 54. During all the years of operation, 1977, 1978, and 1979 before the owners got busted for income tax evasion because they denied entrance to President Carter's Chief of Staff and his date, I went to Studio 54 once a week, as a regular visitor. I cannot disclose all the details but everything you have probably heard about Studio 54 likely happened. I also went to other clubs including Xenon disco, Regine's which reviewers have called the only elegant club in New York City, and El Morocco, as well as others.

To help me raise the capital that I needed to build a taxi fleet, my first wife, a pediatrician and also a Karen, became a lender. She volunteered to lend me $85,000.00 which came from the payout of a life insurance policy following the suicide death of the first wife, a psychiatrist, of her new husband, a world-renowned endocrinologist.

The new $85,000.00 infusion of capital allowed me to meet my initial goals of increasing to a fleet of 22 cabs worth $1,000,000.00, in part due to the inflation of the medallions, by the end of the summer of 1978, my 30th year.

I competed with the big taxi fleets for the available pool of drivers. Working for a big fleet meant that the driver had to belong to a union and get paid 43% of the meter plus tips. Drivers who worked for me rented the cab for a 12-hour shift and kept everything for themselves beyond the fee for the shift and the cost of their gas, making them independent contractors as well as entrepreneurs.

This system, known as horse hiring, started out as illegal but became legal thanks to me. In every vehicle I put an AM/FM radio with cassette player and stereo speakers with no rooftop ads or partitions. These features made the drivers feel as though they had their own personal cab to drive, making it possible for me to attract quality drivers. During the years I drove 16-hour days I listened to every available book from the Books on Tape series available to rent through the mail. This provided me with the opportunity to always expand my mind even while working. I learned about many subjects to which I would otherwise never have gotten exposed. This adheres to my philosophy of always expanding my mind.

The night of John Lennon's death, December 8, 1980, I had picked up a leftover cab to drive. I heard the announcement on the radio when only two blocks away from his residence at The Dakota. I drove over there and followed the ambulance to the emergency room at Roosevelt Hospital. What a night! I still remember the ambulance parked in front of the emergency entrance, empty with all the doors open. When I went back to The Dakota within an hour, police had blocked off the street because of the crowds that formed.

After establishing my taxi fleet in 1978, I started a great new social life. I went to many charity parties and met loads of people over the years. I dated the girl in the national billboard Coppertone ad. I dated another girl, a cover girl for Cosmopolitan, who told me that she had descended from Mary Queen of Scotts. I also dated Susan Hatfield, related to the family of the Hatfield-McCoy feud. I even dated an attractive Chechnyan girl who I met in my cab who I think may have come to New York to raise money for the Chechnyan rebels. I dated a few Mayflower descendants. One girl who I met at a Manhattan party told me that her father served as an SS major in World War II. She said her father would probably kill her if she married a Jew – I asked. She lived at the Delmonico Hotel at 58th Street and Park Avenue. I once dated a beautiful freshman at Manhattan College, over 20 years my junior. One night when I took her dancing at Regine's, mob boss John Gotti and his crew spent the whole night watching her dance moves on the dance floor. I dated a divorcee, first runner-up for the Miss America pageant, in the late 1970's. On our first date we asked each other the reason for divorcing. She did not want children but her husband did. My immediate ex-wife did not want children, but I did. We had an awkward moment in the conversation. Her ex, a Harvard medical school graduate, wrote many medical dramas often turned into movies as well as best-selling books. She got a very good settlement and lived on Park Avenue.

In 1980 or 1981, two of my actress girlfriends wanted me to study acting. I started going to classes with Robert X. Modica at his studio in the building housing Carnegie Hall.

For one of my memorable parties I double dated with Huntington Hartford to a Ford Modeling Agency Christmas party. Hunt co-owned the agency. What a collection of face girls! They kept bumping into me on the dance floor – what a mosh pit.

In those years I fell in with some of the upper class Euro trash crowd. We frequently visited the French Riviera in the summer, a place I have visited on and off for 50 years. With the upper class Euro trash crowd, I had lunch about twice a week at Le Relais, a French restaurant at 63rd and Madison. Over the years, with my Paris-born countess girlfriend, Pascal, who had a friendship with the owner, we held court there. Her father chaired Amax, the largest mining company in the world. They owned homes in Greenwich, CT, and other locations. At Le Relais, we would save one or several seats at the center table for people that we knew or liked, as an example, for the grandson of Generalissimo Franco,

40-year dictator of Spain.

In the early 1990's at Le Relais I met O. J. Simpson, with both of us standing at the bar waiting for our dates. He had come to New York City as part of his work as an NBC football commentator. We talked about USC football and I thanked him for taking USC to the Rose Bowl during my years as a student at USC. I laughingly complained about having to come back from skiing in Aspen six days before school started three years in a row to attend the Rose Bowl game with USC playing. When O.J. played football for USC, they literally gave him the ball to run for virtually every play of the game. They called the USC football team, "The Cardiac Kids," as they always found a way to win, often in the last minutes of the game. Many a year we ruined UCLA and Stanford's attempted bowl bids.

While talking to O.J., I noticed Patty Hearst sitting at a table with friends. I had met her previously at a charity ball in New York, so I introduced her to O.J. Simpson. I should have thanked her because I owned a newspaper distributorship for one of her father's many newspapers, The Los Angeles Herald Examiner, one of my three businesses that helped put me through college. Later O.J. would have the same defense attorney, F. Lee Bailey, who also defended Patty at her 1976 bank robbery trial, in both cases with legal consultant Alan Dershowitz.

As I introduced the two of them, I introduced one of the most notorious people of the 1970's to one of the most notorious people of the 1990's.

Patty Hearst, the granddaughter of William Randolph Hearst, the newspaper magnate and builder of the Hearst Castle in California, had gotten kidnapped as a 19-year-old student at the University of California at Berkeley by the Symbionese Liberation Army in the San Francisco Bay area in February 1974. After keeping her blindfolded in a closet as a prisoner for weeks, except for meals, members of the Symbionese Liberation Army members convinced Patty to join them and help them rob banks as well as commit other crimes. She has had Stockholm syndrome applied to her case, where the prisoner identifies with the captors. The court convicted her of bank robbery and sent her to prison. President Jimmy Carter commuted her sentence to the 22 months' time served and President Bill Clinton issued a pardon to her on his last day in office, January 20, 2001.

As part of the radical environment at University of California at Berkeley prior to Patty Hearst's kidnapping, the man who later became the Unabomber, Ted Kaczynsky, a mathematical prodigy, taught there for two years starting at age 25 in 1967 as an assistant professor. He became the target of one of the most expensive investigations ever conducted by the FBI. On April 3, 1996, the FBI arrested Theodore (Ted) Kaczynski, the Unabomber. He had entered Harvard at age 16 from which he received a bachelor's degree in mathematics and went on to obtain a PhD in mathematics from the University of Michigan. His brother's wife read his Manifesto online and recognized phrases that Ted frequently used. She insisted that her husband read it also, and after reading the Manifesto her husband contacted the FBI.

In 1968, my colonel in the U.S. Army advised me to go to USC and not to University of California at Berkeley, although both schools had accepted me, because of the notoriously radical environment at Berkeley. It made an easy call for me.

My former girlfriend, a French countess of NYC, Greenwich, CT, and Paris. We held court for America's Euro-Trash elite

Photo Caption for Smith girlfriend late seventies

My girlfriend who had attended Smith College, from the late 1970's, with photo taken 30 years later. We went to Studio 54 frequently during its heyday.

I mention this only because Nancy Reagan, a Smith graduate, recommended that her husband, Ronald Reagan, choose George H. W. Bush for his vice president in 1980 among other reasons because Barbara Bush also graduated from Smith College

Chapter 21
East Coast Boat Stories

In the summer of 1978, I bought a fast, 18-foot speedboat that went 48 miles an hour. I enjoyed that boat for 12 years. I took many of my dates out on the water. I preferred picnics floating on the East River behind the United Nations or near the Statue of liberty. I also went up the Hudson River, an hour's boat ride, near the Sing Sing prison where you could see the prisoners. I had picnics in front of Sing Sing, and went swimming near the boat, drifting on slow current down the river. The term "going up the river" must have originated in the Sing Sing prison location up the Hudson River from New York City.

Once some plastic got wrapped around the propeller of my speedboat which shut the engine off from overheating. The boat drifted onto Riker's Island, a New York City correctional facility. A phalanx of officers greeted me with guns drawn. Naturally I talked my way out of that, even getting a tour of Riker's.

When I took one date out on my boat for an afternoon lunch at the River Café to the side of the Brooklyn Bridge, we double docked. As she stepped from one boat to the next to get to the dock, the boats separated, and she fell into the water. The waiters came rushing out to help. Everyone cheered when we walked in to have lunch. Her father had the number one or number two spot in the Polish communist party. I thought of her as a "party" girl. You could always hear the clicks on the phone when I called her — wiretaps I guess.

The people who had the authority in the East European Communist countries in the late 1970's seemed happy to send their kids out of there, 13 years before the collapse.

In 1989 after my speedboat practically sank just from sitting there,

I pumped it out and traded it in for a 31-foot Slickcraft cabin cruiser. In one memorable trip I took it through the ocean, leaving it in Newport, Rhode Island, for a week. I took the train home to New York City, and came back the next week, when I took the boat up to Plymouth, Massachusetts, and historic Boston Harbor. Leaving Boston I hit a lot of fog going north on the coast of Massachusetts. As I did not have radar I had to navigate up the New England coast using a road map plus sonar depth finding to maintain the distance from shore.

By the time I got to the end of the fog I had gotten to the start of New Hampshire. In the far distance across the water you could see Maine, specifically Kennebunkport where I wanted to go. While I planned to stop eventually, just to see what the Secret Service would do, I drove 35 mph in the open ocean straight toward the oceanfront home of Present George Herbert Walker Bush in the first summer of his presidency. I planned to stop eventually.

The U. S. Navy/Secret Service scrambled an interceptor boat from the Navy ship anchored in the ocean in front of the president's home, to cut me off. When I realized their concern, I slowed down, waved, and pulled out a camera to take a picture. Seeing me as not a threat, they backed off.

After fueling up I left Kennebunkport in the late afternoon. I needed to get to the Cape Cod Canal which led onto Woods Hole before dark. With the route I chose, I had no sight of land for 1 ½ hours at 35 mph, navigating by compass. I got there. At Woods Hole, because of heavy riptides, I had a difficult dock but mastered it. I left the boat and went back to New York by train. I sent my accountant to pick up the boat and bring it back to New York.

My cabin cruiser
1989

My speedboat in NYC
Great for picnics in
Long Island Sound
floating in front of
United Nations, Statue
of Liberty or Sing Sing
Prison.

Chapter 22
Adventures in Running My Taxi Business

Although I lived near a taxi stand at West 10th Street and Sixth Avenue, I would dispatch from my apartment building, the first building next to the post office on the corner.

Once when dispatching on the street corner, a lady asked me if I worked for the Secret Service because the President's son, Ron Reagan, lived 100 yards away on my block.

Whenever a driver picked up a cab, he or she needed to check the oil and the transmission oil before accepting the cab for the shift. Otherwise the vehicle could stop in the middle of the shift if it ran out of oil. The shifts changed at 6:00 a.m. and at 6:00 p.m. After checking the oil, the driver had to close the hood which made a loud, banging sound. The neighbors complained. The landlord loved it because it contributed to having irate tenants move out of the rent-controlled apartment, allowing the owner to increase the rent. Tenants from the NYU Law School used legal means to seize control of the building from the owner. They sent me an eviction notice. This put me under pressure to move out.

Once I moved out, I could quash the eviction. I sublet the apartment to one of my drivers, a former POW in Korea for six months in the 1950's, who continued to live there for six years until he died in the apartment. When the County asked me if I knew anything about him, I told them he had served in the U. S. Army during the Korean War. After receiving that information, they had his remains buried in the VA Cemetery instead of in Potter's Field. I got all the money back that I paid for rent plus a small profit. I used that address as my fleet address. The tenant brought the mail to me every day on weekdays to wherever

I dispatched cabs from at the time, including my future garage.

I also had a Bay of Pigs POW work for me. I had top leaders of Afghanistan drive my cabs in the 1980's. I had physicians from Europe and Africa drive my cabs while waiting to get U. S. licensing as well as many Broadway and movie actors. I had one retired sea captain drive my cabs. I could attract this eclectic mix of high end drivers by wording my ads in the newspaper on a personal level to drive my personal taxicabs that had AM-FM stereo systems, no partitions, and no roof-top advertising, unlike the union taxi fleet vehicles. Each of my taxis had a spare tire and a jack so that the driver could quickly change a flat and get back to work. The union cabs would often wait up to four hours for a tire change. The union taxi fleets had no radios, roof-top advertising, and partitions, which cut down on the driver's tips. The driver of one of my cabs could feel pride in driving a quality car. My drivers became true entrepreneurs with a quality life.

After I had a garage I would buy $100 boxes of toilet paper for the two bathrooms. I put the word out that any cab driver in the city could stop at my garage in the heart of midtown Manhattan to use the toilet. I would try to get any driver not already working for me to come and work for me. I had the highest percentage of cabs dispatched of any fleet in the city.

Once after landing at JFK Airport after 24 hours of flying home from travel, I went to the cab line and found one of my cabs had just broken down. I found another of my 51 cabs also in line. I took my working cab, let my driver become my passenger, and pushed my broken cab all the way to my garage on West 53rd St. We saved the driver's day and a $50 tow charge.

Another time, while dispatching cabs from my apartment on West 10th St., I finished the evening shift change and had a cab with no brakes and another with a not-working engine. I used one to push the other to the West Side repair shop saving two shifts and two tow charges.

Once I had to get two repaired cabs from a Midtown West repair shop to the Village for a shift change. I took one cab and on the street I asked a potential hailing fare from Texas if he would drive my other cab downtown for a free ride. Somewhere in Texas lives a man who had the story of visiting NYC and getting to drive a taxi.

To get my fleet up to 51 cabs I used the equity which grew as existing cabs went up in value plus my earnings while driving one of the cabs.

In 2010, when riding in a taxi in Manhattan, years after I had stopped running cabs, the driver recognized me and said: "You were the best boss I ever had."

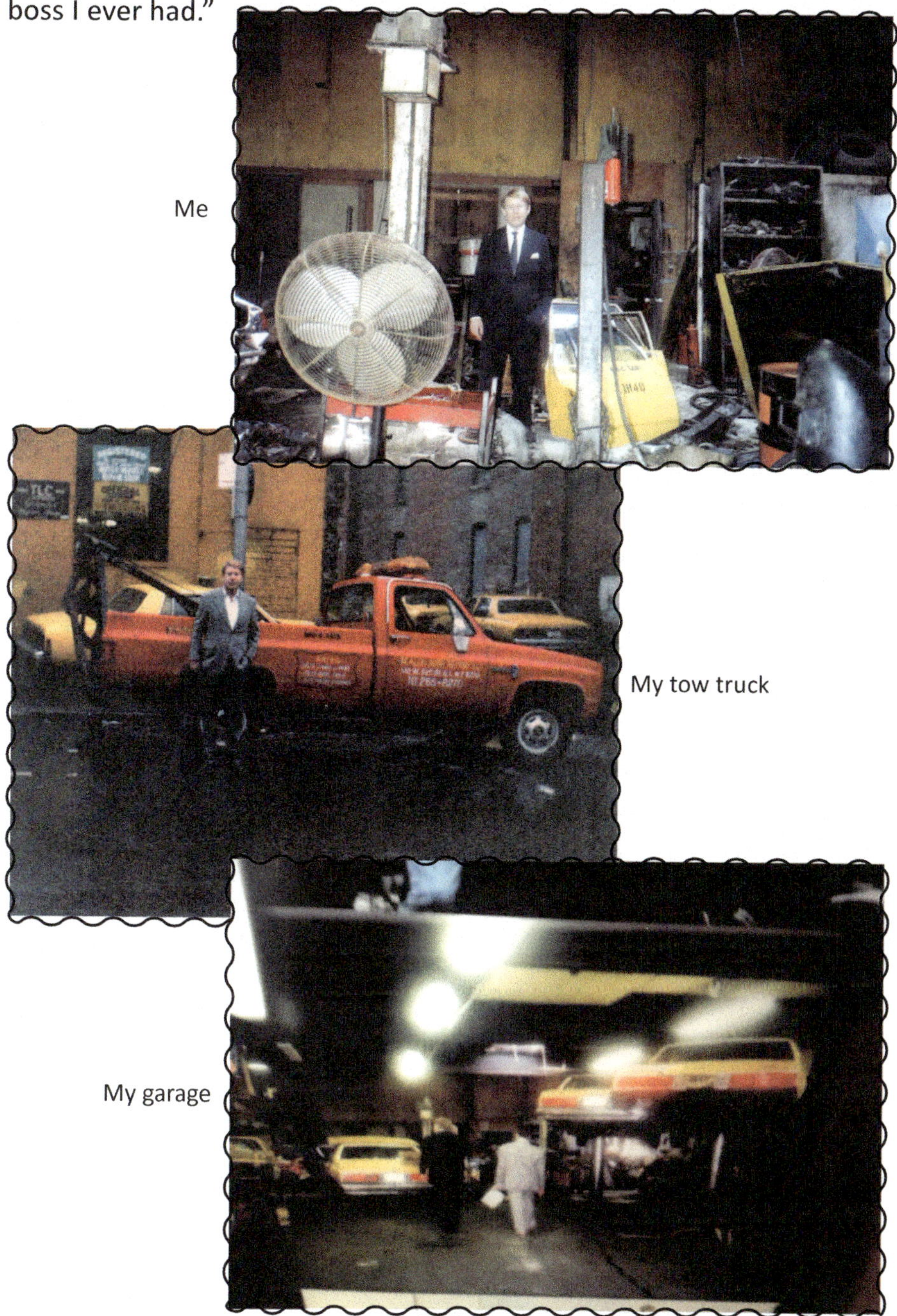

Me

My tow truck

My garage

Chapter 23
Five-Star Living Plus Third-World Travel

At age 35 I married on the rebound a fun girl, Diane, who wanted to become a U. S. Senator. I wanted out after the initial proposal and decided to require an iron-tight prenuptual agreement, thinking that would end it. To my surprise, she agreed to sign the prenup, and we married a month later. For advice to fellow hot shot readers, when in doubt just break off the relationship and do not try to impose a hard-ass prenuptual agreement.

Unbeknownst to anyone but me I had found myself under a high level of pressure to move out of my apartment in Greenwich Village as I had gotten an eviction notice because of the noise created at the change of shift of my taxicabs in front of the apartment building at 6:00 am and 6:00 pm every day.

When Diane and I married, I moved into her large, pre-war rent controlled apartment at 79th and Second Ave. on the Upper East Side of Manhattan. Simultaneously, I moved the taxicab shift-change for my 36 cabs from in front of my Greenwich Village apartment to the nearby cab stand of my new home uptown.

In her really large, pre-war, rent-controlled Manhattan apartment we had a New Year's Eve party every New Year's Eve for each of the six years of our marriage, mostly attended by other taxi fleet owners and our personal friends, one of the biggest events on the Upper East Side often with 65 guests. We filled the bathtub with ice and bottles of champagne. We hired Broadway actors looking for extra income to serve as waiters and bartenders.

During the next six years she and I went on about a trip a year together. We went to Europe on a grand tour. We went to California and Nevada twice. In 1987, she went with me to a taxi fleet owners' convention in Las Vegas where Coach Tarkanian, "the shark," a world-famous basketball coach and motivational speaker gave a memorable speech at our meeting at the Riviera Hotel and Casino. At the time I owned 51 taxicabs. One summer, we went on a driving trip north of Lake Superior into Canada.

When I traveled with my wife, she preferred to stay at five-star hotels. We had a suite at the Hotel de Crillon in the Place de la Concorde in Paris, which first opened in 1758. They had a plaque on the door of the suite two doors down from ours stating that U. S. President Woodrow Wilson lived there for the month of January in 1919 while preparing the Treaty of Versailles. We stayed at the Carlton Hotel in Cannes, France and the Hotel de Paris in Monaco. We stayed in the Villa d'Este Suite at the Hotel Portofino, in Portofino, Italy, where a phone call to New York to manage my taxi fleet cost $300.00.

Whenever I went to London I stayed at Five-Star hotels including Claridge's Hotel in the Anne Getty Suite, the Connaught Hotel, or the Park Lane Hotel.

During my marriage, I traveled on my own in third world countries, not preferred by my wife. I traveled on my own on many trips throughout the world having many adventures.

I can mention one trip going from Liberia to Sierra Leon in my car with two guards/drivers. At the border crossing I put my cash in my socks as you couldn't trust the border guards not to steal from you at any border crossing. While waiting I went into a room where my two guards had their shoes off for a search, but the border guards failed to search me. It placed a tourist at risk for loss of life. Potentially, they could take your cash and bury you out back. From then on, I decided not to cross African borders other than by airplane.

Starting the day after the election of President George H. W. Bush in 1988, I took off on an around-the-world scuba diving trip for 18 days. I spent the first night in Las Vegas. I spent the second night in the Beverly Hills Hotel on Sunset Boulevard in Suite 12B where, by report, JFK rendezvoused with Marilyn Monroe many times during his presidency.

Next I stopped in Hawaii, followed by a brief stop at Johnston Atoll, where America keeps its poison gas supply, and where they did not allow tourists to disembark the airplane. I went on to scuba dive the

Jap Navy on the bottom of the Truk Lagoon.

At the next stop, Palau, I met a troop of traveling doctors and nurses who did free plastic surgery for third world citizens in different countries several months a year. They felt glad to meet a travelling American. Palau had excellent scuba diving and even greater social experiences. I passed through the Philippines on my way to Singapore. I had a complete tour by limousine of Sri Lanka, formally Ceylon, before going on to the Maldives for more scuba. I stopped in Bombay where I toured the Gandhi house. From there I got back to NYC in 24 hours with a transfer in Amsterdam.

At the end of November 1988, I took Pan Am Flight 103 from Amsterdam to JFK exactly three weeks before Libyans bombed the same flight causing the aircraft to explode in midair one hour after departure, over Lockerbie, Scotland.

Second marriage day

Chapter 24
Famous People Who Crossed My Path

To get up to 51 taxicabs I used my earnings while driving one of the cabs plus the equity in the medallions that I owned, which grew as existing medallions went up in value.

While driving a taxicab I met many famous people and had interesting conversations with them. With the charity parties I attended and my travels, now up to 150 countries, I have created a very eclectic list of famous people with whom I have had some kind of interaction.

Mayor Ed Koch (NYC)	Ben Gazzara	Amarillo Slim
Mayor Rudy Giuliani (NYC)	Mike Wallace	Andrea McArdle
Att. Gen, Ramsey Clark	Jim Jensen	Tommy Tune
John Chancellor	Robert DeNiro	Andy Rooney
Johnny Weissmuller	Gov. Pataki (NY)	Harry Reasoner
Walter Matthau	Sen. Richard Bryan (NV)	Al Roker
Art Linkletter	Sen. Harry Reid (NV)	Rick Barry
Carl Sagan	Norton Simon	Barry Farber
Joe Franklin	Geraldo Rivera	Sandy Dennis
Robin Leach	David Rockefeller	Barry Gray
Norm McDonald	Ruth Messenger	John Stossel
Dustin Hoffman (3)	Mort Zuckerman	Betty Friedan
Fay Dunaway		
Huntington Hartford	Ray Milland	Dennis Thatcher
Clive Barnes	Andy Warhol	Bella Abzug
Woody Allen (2)	O.J. Simpson	VP Al Gore
Mia Farrow (2)	Wilford Brimley	Arthur Schlesinger
Sen. Daniel P. Moynihan (NY)	Jerry Lewis	Stephen Baldwin
Warren Beatty	Geoffrey Holder	Mary Travers
Diane Keaton (3)		Hermione Gingold
Doyle Brunson	Nicholas Cage	John Voight
Trixie (Honeymooners)	James Woods	Matt Damon

Johnny Moss	Leonard Nimoy	Harmon Killebrew
Lorraine Newman	Annabelle Sicora	F. Murray Abraham
Ally Sheedy	Patrick O'Neill	Tom Sellek
Gilda Radner	Claire Bloom	Joel Grey
William Hurt	Art Garfunkel	Lynn Redgrave
Paul, Linda, Stella McCartney	Monica Seles	David Koch
Tony Randall	Regis Philbin	Joe Montana
Kirk Douglas	Mary Tyler Moore	Roy Schneider
Rep. Shelley Berkley (D-NV)	Tony Curtis	Roger Penske
Paul Begala	Sen. John Ensign (NV)	James Carville
Pres. Bill Clinton	Sen. John McCain (AZ)	Bruce Willis
Susan Sarandon	Sen. Dean Heller (NV)	Grover Norquist
BB King	Ben Stein	

<u>Andy Rooney</u>: anchor for CBS's Sixty Minutes. I met him in my taxi

<u>Governor George Pataki</u>, during the eight years that he served as New State Governor: social event at the Waldorf

<u>Senator Richard Bryan</u>, former Nevada governor and at the time, current Democratic U. S. Senator from Nevada, and chairman of the Senate Intelligence Committee: my wife and I had a two-hour luncheon with him three days before he announced his retirement from politics at age 61. We tried desperately to talk him out of it but to no avail.

<u>Harry Reid</u>, Democratic Senior Senator from Nevada: I met him twice at political fundraisers. He told me that he doubted the ability of the then-candidate-for-president, George W. Bush, to make good decisions.

<u>Norton Simon</u>, entrepreneur, owner of large art museums in West Palm Beach and Pasadena, unsuccessful candidate as a Republican for the U. S. Senate in California, now deceased: I met him in my taxi. He felt beside himself with joy that a New York cab driver recognized him. It more than made his day, it made his life.

<u>Geraldo Rivera</u>, Fox New commentator: he interviewed me as one of the players at a Las Vegas poker tournament.

<u>Ben Gazzara</u>, actor in many TV series: I met him in my cab and took him co-op (apartment) hunting.

<u>Mike Wallace</u>, anchor of CBS's Sixty Minutes: I met him in my cab, told him of the corruption in the taxi industry and my position as a fleet owner. He offered to expose them if I would appear on his show but I had to decline for reasons of self-preservation.

112

<u>Al Roker</u>, weatherman for the NBC Today Show: I chatted with him at the hot dog stand in front of Rockefeller Center where we had each gone to get a hot dog.

<u>Rick Barry</u>, professional basketball player.

<u>Amarillo Slim</u>, who won two World Series of Poker in the 1970's: we chatted over the years while playing poker.

<u>Johnny Weissmuller</u>, the original Tarzan: I delivered his newspaper in Ft. Lauderdale and collected only from him in person. I delivered a bill to everyone else with a newspaper.

<u>Walter Matthau</u>, actor: I met him in a theater at a play we both attended.

<u>Art Linkletter</u>, national TV host: we sat next to each other at a Broadway play. He confirmed that he stayed at the houseboat in Srinagar, Kashmir, where I stayed immediately after him as a 20-year-old in the Army. I lent him my pen to sign autographs during the intermission.

<u>Carl Sagan</u>, astronomer and TV personality ("The Cosmos"): his wife accompanied him in my cab. Very friendly.

<u>Robin Leach</u>, "Lifestyles of the Rich and Famous:" we met at Au Bar nightclub, introduced by my date, Valerie Jennings, Peter's first wife.

<u>David Rockefeller</u>, CEO of Chase Manhattan Bank: he came to one of the training classes in which I participated at the Chase Manhattan Bank International Training Lending Program, just before I started buying taxis. When he asked for questions, I asked: "What is your plan to surpass Citibank in size in the future?"

<u>Ruth Messinger</u>, losing candidate for mayor of New York City: we met at a party during her candidacy.

<u>Margaret Thatcher</u>, Former British Prime Minister: in my cab from the theater district in the evening with her husband, Dennis Thatcher. We talked about where they now live and the status of certain New York hotels. We got stuck in traffic by Grand Central Station for about three minutes. She became very uneasy, as did her husband, as she had no security coverage. I kept an eye out for assassins. When we reached their hotel near the United Nations, she dashed out of the cab and into the hotel while her congenial husband paid the bill.

<u>Vice President Al Gore</u>, at a political function at Bally's Hotel and Casino in Las Vegas, before he began running for U. S. President: I shook his hand. I should have told him to watch out for the defective printing

of the Palm Beach County ballots.

U.S. Senator Daniel P. Moynihan, Democrat, New York: we met in my taxi. We drove up Third Avenue in my taxi to take the Triboro Bridge to La Guardia Airport. Regarding the two government-funded skyscraper apartments along the route in Harlem, sitting completely empty since completion four or five years previously, I chewed his ear off for 20 minutes about this. Wouldn't you know, within two months, those apartment buildings had opened to receive tenants. Now do you believe that I ran Thailand for the U.S. Army as a colonel's aide?

Harmon Killebrew, a Hall of Fame professional baseball player: I played golf with him at a charity event.

Ally Sheedy, actress (in "The Breakfast Club"): I met and talked with her in Central Park where we both brought our children to play.

Tom Selleck, actor: we met while walking on Madison Avenue. I belonged to Kappa Alpha and he belonged to Sigma Chi fraternity at USC. We had a very friendly conversation about that life back in the day.

Eugene McCarthy, Democratic U. S. Sen. from Minnesota, who ran for the United States Presidency in 1968, known as "clean Gene": we had a pleasant conversation while taking him to the airport in my taxi.

Jason Robards, actor: a very friendly person. Did you know that he served in the U. S. Navy at Pearl Harbor during the attack on Pearl Harbor on December 7, 1941?

Betty Friedan, feminist author and lecturer: I used to hang with her and her medical student daughter on the Cunard ship Queen Elizabeth during the Silver Jubilee of Her Majesty's reign where the British Navy greeted our ship over a 50-mile entrance way to the Southampton docking with 21 gun salutes.

Huntington Hartford, a friend: I often visited his 1 Beekman Place mansion with friends. On many occasions, he showed me new games that he had invented. He part owned the Ford Modeling Agency. We double dated to the agency Christmas party one year.

Mia Farrow, actress: I once picked her up in my cab alone and mentioned in a friendly conversation that she and Woody Allen had ridden in my cab in the past while making out. She responded in a laughing way that she wished I had warned her about him.

Diane Keaton, actress: I met her three times, the last time when she and Warren Beatty rode in my cab on a date. She always acted very friendly.

Lorraine Newman, comedian: in late September 1976 I met her in my cab. She said she had a tip for me, to watch a new comedy show coming out the following week called Saturday Night Live.

O.J. Simpson, professional football player and NBC announcer for football games: as we both waited for our dates at the bar at Le Relais restaurant at 63rd St. and Madison Avenue, the power lunch place for the Eurotrash crowd, I introduced myself. I thanked him for USC football and our many Rose Bowl game appearances during his time on the team. I saw Patty Hearst sitting at a table nearby, and I introduced him to her. I actually introduced the number one fugitive of the 1970s to the number one fugitive, though briefly, of the 1990s. This took place slightly before the murders.

Dustin Hoffman, actor: he rode in my tab three times, very friendly.

Ray Milland, British actor in the 1940's and 1950's: in 1977, we shared seating arrangements on a delayed flight from Madrid to Malaga, Spain, where he lived. We spent about three hours together chatting about old Hollywood, with him about age 75 and me on my way to Africa.

Nicholas Cage, actor: I took him and his very hot girlfriend around Manhattan in my cab looking at a list of places he might consider living if he moved to Manhattan, in a very fun hour.

Andy Warhol, artist, photographer, editor of "Interview Magazine": I met Andy several times at Studio 54. One charity event hosted by Brooke Shields and Elizabeth Taylor at the Pierre Hotel stood out. At a table for four, he and his date sat with me and my date for the three hours of the event. He mostly stayed at the table because everyone came up to him. Everybody knew Andy. As the founder of Interview Magazine, he had a camera with him that he used from time to time to take pictures of people there.

Joel Gray, actor and vocalist: I met him at a theater in London after a play that we both attended -- a very friendly guy.

William Hurt, actor: I met him in the process of his moving out of an apartment at 77th and Amsterdam where my then girlfriend moved in, essentially simultaneously. This girlfriend, Paula, in the late 1970's went with me to the top New York City nightclubs such as Studio 54,

El Morocco, or Xenon's on Friday or Saturday night. Paula would spend the other weekend night with her other boyfriend in the governor's mansion of a nearby state, where he lived with his parents, the governor and his wife. We originally met at a Smith-Seven Sisters mixer. She went on to obtain her MBA from NYU.

Paul McCartney, one of the Beatles: in 1975 when I still had just one cab, I picked him up in my Checker taxi as I pulled out of the Hilton on Sixth Avenue at 54th St. he ran up to my cab, stuck his head in the window, and asked: "Are you free?" I recognized him immediately and answered, "For you, any time." To avoid unwanted public attention, he, together with his wife Linda and daughter Stella, had a habit of hailing a taxi across the street from the hotel where they stayed in New York, the Warwick Hotel in the Cary Grant suite. The Beatles always stayed at the Warwick Hotel in the Cary Grant suite when they came to New York City to perform at Carnegie Hall and on the Ed Sullivan show. Paul had a very friendly manner. Twenty-five years later, together with my wife, our six-month-old twin sons, and our traveling nanny we also stayed in the Cary Grant suite in the Warwick Hotel for a few days.

David Koch, at the time, the richest bachelor on the planet: introduced by a mutual friend trying to impress me by who she knew at the Metropolitan Opera. I had not yet started dating his former girlfriend. We once traveled to Nassau for a long weekend and stayed in her friend's mansion, the one just above the estate of the prime minister of the Bahamas.

Tony Randall, actor: we met at a party at the Waldorf Astoria Hotel. Very friendly.

Mary Tyler Moore, actress: I kept running into her walking in the streets of the upper East Side of Manhattan. We spoke several times.

Shelley Berkeley, our Nevada Congresswoman: she had her office in our building. We became friends. She offered to assist in having the U.S. government help in finding my two lost/stolen/missing children. As a summer intern when a college student, my son Eric worked at the U. S. State Department when still on the list of Missing Children.

Gennifer Flowers, vocalist and friend of President Bill Clinton: we lived in the same guard-gated community in Las Vegas, four houses away from where she lived with her husband. We talked on the street from time to time.

<u>Tony Curtis</u>, actor: we met at a society party in Las Vegas.

<u>Roger Penske</u>, racecar sponsor and truck rental company owner: I met him while looking at his Ferrari collection on display at the Wynn hotel in Las Vegas. He introduced himself to me.

<u>Paul Begala</u>, Democratic Party spokesman: we met at a political event sponsored by Senator Harry Reid in Nevada.

<u>James Carvel</u>, Democratic/Clinton spokesman and professor at Tulane University where my daughter Lara attends: we met and talked on the casino floor of the Wynn Hotel and Casino in Las Vegas.

<u>President Bill Clinton</u>: we met at an Oil Independence Conference in Las Vegas sponsored by Nevada Senator Harry Reid. We shook hands.

<u>U. S. Senator John Ensign</u>, Republican, Nevada: I spoke to him at an Asian Business Development fundraising luncheon in Las Vegas. He talked about going to Iowa for presidential exploration talks. Within a month, the sex scandal broke. He has gone back to working as a veterinarian.

<u>U. S. Senator John McCain</u>, Republican, Arizona: we met at a political event in Las Vegas during his campaign for president.

<u>U. S. Senator Dean Heller</u>, Republican, Nevada: we met at a political fundraiser for him in Las Vegas where those who paid an extra fee had the right to mingle with the senator in a separate room before he gave his talk. When I mentioned USC and my fraternity, he wanted to talk about old memories of USC and his fraternity, two houses down from my fraternity on the fraternity row. Since this took up time from fundraising activities, after 20 minutes his staff members came to redirect him to speak with others present.

<u>Grover Norquist</u>, Republican anti-new tax strategist: we met at a political fundraiser in Las Vegas where he gave the keynote speech.

<u>BB King</u>, musician: we lived in the same complex in Las Vegas, but we met and spoke amicably at the local Postal Service store about his upcoming performances.

<u>Susan Sarandon</u>, actress: my son Charles and I recognized and chatted with her in a clothing store in new York City. When I mentioned that he felt interested in becoming an actor, she gave some helpful advice.

<u>Ben Stein</u>, professor, political commentator, and actor: we met at a building in Washington, D.C., where he works. My son Charles

remembered that he played the role of a teacher in the film, "Ferris Bueller's Day Off."

U. S. Senator Ted Cruz, Republican, Texas: we met at a political rally in Las Vegas.

Poker buddies I met in my tournament days: Wilford Brimley, Johnny Moss, Norm McDonald, and James Wood.

I also met the following celebrities briefly, with light conversation in my taxi:

John Chancellor, NBC national news anchor

Jim Jensen, local TV news anchor

Robert DeNiro, actor

Harry Reasoner, ABC national news anchor

Barry Farber, local and national radio host

Sandy Dennis, a female film and stage actress

Andrea McArdle, who played Annie on Broadway

Tommy Tune, Broadway star

Joe Franklin, national radio host

Mark Zuckerman, owner of the New York Daily News, among other businesses

Bella Abzug, an outspoken New York U. S. Congresswoman, very friendly

Arthur Schlesinger, author who worked with President Kennedy

Mary Travers, of the music group Peter, Paul, and Mary, very friendly

Hermione Gingold, actress

F. Murray Abraham, actor

Patrick O'Neill, actor

Barry Gray, national radio host

John Stossel, TV host on Fox network

Clive Barnes, New York Times theater critic

Warren Beatty, actor

Trixie, from the Honeymooners (a famous TV show starring Jackie Gleason in the 1950s)

Anabella Sciorra, actress

Leonard Nimoy who played Mr. Spock in Star Trek

Geoffrey Holder, actor

Jerry Lewis, comedian

Stephen Baldwin, actor

Jeff Jeffries, actor
Faye Dunaway, actress
Gilda Radner, actress/comedian
Claire Bloom, actress
Art Garfunkel, singer
Lynn Redgrave, actress
Monica Seles, tennis player
Roy Schneider, actor

My Russian girlfriend who I saved from drowning in Long Island Sound. This is what you have to look like to get an exit visa from the Soviet Union to Israel in 1976. Don't tell anyone but she really wasn't Jewish

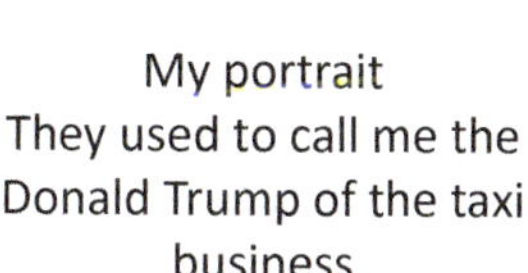

My portrait
They used to call me the Donald Trump of the taxi business

Another Karen
in my life

She was also dating
David Kock,
the world's richest
bachelor

Chapter 25
Starting and Maintaining a Taxi Company in New York City

Nineteen years after coming to New York City after college with only $75 in my pocket I had 51 taxicabs (one-half of 1% of all the taxicabs in New York City. Like the song says, Living on an American Express Card, which I did, for two months. How could I do such a thing? I drove a taxi and then purchased a taxi while borrowing money however I could. Our liberal Congress passed a law to guarantee loans to minority citizens who needed to borrow money to start a business, with a rider added to the bill to include Vietnam Era War veterans.

Did I mention that on leaving the Army our flight left Bangkok on September 6, 1968 and landed at the airport in Saigon for 15 minutes on the way to Clark Air Force Base in the Philippines? That stop in Vietnam made me a Vietnam vet and made all my pay and back pay tax free.

U.S. government backed SBIC loans made by private investors allowed me to purchase the second half of my taxi medallion fleet. Getting tens of millions of dollars in government backed loans because of the Vietnam War likely made me the highest remunerated Vietnam Era veteran. In some way, I owe my taxi fleet to Ho Chi Minh.

In 1985 I had 35 cabs operating out of a long cab stand at 78th Street and Lexington. One evening as I dispatched my cabs from the front seat of one of my cabs, with a long line of drivers waiting for their keys as usual, all of a sudden four cop cars came rushing in, halting all traffic. It seemed that some local resident had reported a possible drug selling operation going on, with people seen handing over money and receiving something, in this case, car keys. It made for quite a scene but I quickly proved my innocence. The local residents objected to the commotion associated with a perfectly efficient system, forcing me to buy a garage at 542 W 53rd St. This whole situation eventually led to the Taxi and Limousine Commission making a new rule forbidding fleets from operating out of cab stands.

When I first started owning and operating multiple taxicabs I initiated the practice of horse hiring which at the time the Commission did not allow. When I left the business in 1996 and even today that remains the predominate method in use, among the ways to rent out vehicles by the shift, week, or month. You could say that I personally broke the union.

As to my garage, I bought the stock of the company that owned the perpetual lease of this property from the City of New York. By report, the man I purchased this deal from had bribed the New York City real estate department for this deal. Eventually, he also wanted to get the lucrative inspection station rights for his garage to inspect taxi cabs. He tried to bribe his way into this but got caught. This started my opportunity to purchase his company. To settle, he had to do community service at an AIDS hospice where he contracted AIDS and later died.

With my garage I created a meter shop, body shop, tire repair shop, transmission rebuilding, and motor vehicle repairs of any kind. We changed engines and even the chassis, the steel frame that they build the car on. The deep potholes on Manhattan streets would sometimes result in bending the structure of the chassis making it unrepairable. Manhattan may have had the worst maintained streets in North America. Especially Europeans who rode in my cab would exclaim about the poor condition of the streets. The article in New York Magazine in 1992 where they interviewed me among many others cited that comment about the deep potholes in the streets of Manhattan.

At an industry dinner, I once sat next to the Taxi Commissioner who reported proudly that he had gotten taxi licenses for women out of homeless shelters to help them become employed. I interrupted him to tell him that I had hired such a women as a driver. In the first hour on the first day on the job, after carrying two fares, she took the money, went into a bar, and got drunk. I received a phone call from the bartender who said: "We have your taxi driver here drunk in our bar. You better come and get your cab." The Commissioner's smile disappeared and he never spoke of the program again.

They based the popular TV show, "Taxi," on a Manhattan taxi garage called Sunshine Cab Company. As a sidebar, I had previously named one of my 26 corporations Sunshine Taxi, Inc.

My taxi fleet of 51 cabs had only nine employees on salary plus 266 independent contracted drivers. This compares with other fleets of comparable size that would have up to nineteen salaried employees. After I dispatched all the cabs out every night I would often go around to other fleets and see if they got all their cabs out. I would invariably have the highest ratio of cabs out, with good American friendly management as compared to the competition.

One of my drivers had his cab robbed at gunpoint. Three weeks later an inquisitive neighbor saw the cab parked for several days in a field in the Bronx. I went up to the cab with the driver and dispatched it from the field. After that, I went to the police department to release the car from the stolen car police report. They felt very upset that they didn't get the car first to look for evidence, such as fingerprints. We had known the police to keep a car for evidence for months.

It seems everything rips off the businessman in New York. We smile and laugh out loud every time we see the 2016 TV ads inviting business owners to bring their businesses to the hospitable business environment in New York.

Rush Limbaugh recently stated that he did not even want to spend the night when he came to give a speech in New York as New York State would start auditing him again as it did in the past when he lived and worked there, and which led to his moving to another state

The corruption in the taxi industry had become so widely known that in a sting operation at a taxi inspection station, officers arrested all of the inspectors on duty for taking bribes. We fleet owners laughed because all the inspectors took bribes and they only arrested half. You can't even blame the inspectors. They had the pollution requirements so high that nothing could pass legally without false adjustments. That even went for brand new Chevys right from the dealer. We thought of that when we heard Rachel Madow's May 2016 TV show commenting that many members and leaders of the New York legislature have gone to prison for corruption. We taxi fleet owners had long noted that they passed laws with which no one could comply without paying an administrative fee/tip/bribe.

When I had 22 cabs in the winter of 1979 at age 32 we had the second national fuel crisis with long lines at the gas stations to get fuel. My cabs relied on buying gas on the street. Over that two or three month fuel crisis, I got my fuel from the Mafia. I had my own fuel pump on West 28th Street. Very friendly people, businessmen, just remember to pay them first. A Hot Shot story.

Once when driving a spare cab, I met Mike Wallace of the "60 Minutes" TV show and told him how corrupt the NYC Taxi Commission and EPA inspection system had become. He invited me to come in and tell my story. Sorry, Mike, I couldn't do it then as I was still too close to the business.

Also at the end of the month the local cops would come by my fleet to make their ticket quota as some of my cabs would come in a few minutes before 6:00 pm before they could legally park. In those years, my fleet/taxi commission fines averaged $700 per week, fines given out by recently unemployed, newly-hired-as-taxi-inspectors CITA workers, partially funded by the Federal Government. Their supervisors apparently told them that if they gave enough tickets/fines, they could possibly keep their jobs.

LIST OF NEW YORK CITY TAXI MEDALLIONS OWNED BY NED F. CRUEY

5Y48	5Y49	3H59	3H60	5L48	5L49	4G46
4G50	8H20	8H21	6N62	6N63	6N64	2P94
2P95	2P96	6K55	6K56	2P78	2P79	7K44
7K45	7K46	8L62	8L63	7K47	7K48	7K74
7K75	7K76	7K77	7K78	7K79	7K80	6P64
6P65	1L89	1L90	7G28	7G30	3N44	3N45
1K88	1K89	4H95	4H96	4P95	4P96	5J50
5J51	5J52					

After Fire at my garage on West 53rd Street
New York, NY
June 3, 1996

Chapter 26
The Art of the Deal

In 1988 I read Donald Trump's book "The Art of the Deal" and decided to diversify. I went to Atlantic City and with a broker tried to buy the Resorts Casino by doing a public offering. At that point, I had 26 corporations as back up. They considered selling to me, but just then Merv Griffin bought it for $50 million down. I next tried The Claridge Hotel, at Boardwalk and Park Place in Atlantic City, NJ. Fortunately I did not succeed in the purchase as both these and others dropped in value three-fold over the years.

With no children, I, an only child decided to get a divorce instead, even though I had a blast traveling the world many times on my own throughout the year.

They used to call me the Donald Trump of the taxi business, as a tall blond New York City businessman who wore business suits. It turned out we both applied for a divorce the same month and year using a prenuptual and requiring a trial, both of which ended in the same month 27 months later.

As the only real difference between us, I arrived in NYC with $75 while he started with much larger security backing from his father for his various real estate investments. He has had more financial success, but I too came to NYC to have many companies and then run for President. I have had to happily settle for a great wife and family and arguably the best house with definitely the greatest view in Clark County, Nevada. Our house has such a terrific view that the local Las Vegas Trump organization has had two events in it, including one barbecue as a thank you to the local Trump election workers. We have had three more parties since then with unrelated themes.

In my prenuptual trial that took place over 27 month between 1989 to 1991, the appeals court review resulted in making new New York State case law regarding what one side has to show the other side in a prenuptual trial.

I won the trial. Paying both sides of the legal bill caused me to drop down to 28 cabs.

About this time New York State as well as New York City urgently needed money to pay all of its welfare and other programs. When they announced that they would levy new taxes on the New York Stock Exchange, those in charge of the New York Stock Exchange responded that they would move the stock exchange to New Jersey, if that took place.

New York City taxicabs did not have the option of moving their business to New Jersey. Instead of taxing the New York Stock Exchange, the New York City government decided to levy a new tax, of $2400 per year for Workman's Comp policies per cab, applicable 18 months retroactive. This Workman's Comp tax did not apply anywhere else in the State of New York, only in New York City. The State owned the State Insurance Fund and they could get all the new premiums to fund the State government. This devastating blow to all taxi owners made it impossible to turn a profit anymore.

I had already dropped down to 28 cabs. However, the City of New York wanted me to pay retroactively for Workers Comp premiums to bring myself up to date for cabs I didn't own anymore. That forced me to drop down to 18 cabs and a garage.

Workman's Comp premiums never existed before in the 80 years of taxi cabs in New York City for leased-out cabs. Workman's Comp duplicated existing liability policies. It appeared only to have a goal of providing revenue to the City and State of New York. However, the government had not given the taxi rate structure a raise in nine years. I did not appreciate New York ruining the viability of my business to cover the welfare benefits, $41,000 per family, of all the new immigrants arriving in New York City. When a raise finally came all the fleet owners looked to me for guidance as to how to adjust the shift rate to the drives. Mathematically, I determined that raising the charge to the driver for the 12-hour shift from $75 to $95, or a $20 raise per shift, would make sense. With that $20 increase, after thirteen hours my drivers, who liked me, staged a mini strike. I backed down to $85 per shift charge to the driver, a $10 increase, and the strike ended.

I immediately started to sell more medallions as I knew we would never turn a profit. Take the taxi meters. The Taxi and Limousine Commissioner, Jay Touroff, became a partner in a meter company with a requirement for every New York City taxicab to purchase their $900 meter by a certain date. To change all my cabs to the new meter from the perfectly good existing Swedish meters for which we paid $50 each, cost many, many thousands of dollars. Two weeks before the deadline they allowed one other company to enter the market, which charged $600.

After the installation of the new meters I would have 25% of my cabs in line at the meter shop for meter repair every Monday. The old $50 meters never broke. People would even steal the new meters because of their high cost. Mayor Koch's criminal commissioners had responsibility. It came out that the taxi commissioner who made me get an unneeded garage, owned a major share of the new meter company. He made millions and only got house arrest.

One time, they gave 70 free medallions to a highly connected city-affiliated person to do a diesel fuel study. They got to keep all the revenue for themselves for several years just to test diesel fuel usage for cabs.

Chapter 27
Cute Pediatrician, 31

In the middle of my divorce I changed lawyers to a cheaper one, a female friend. When speaking with her I had lamented my age of 43 and no children. She recommended looking at New York Magazine personal ads for professionals. The magazine had mentioned me once in the fall of 1992 as a mover and shaker in New York, alphabetically right next to Governor Cary.

I saw one personal ad in New York Magazine that stood out: "Cute pediatrician, 31." It sounded good. Having had a previous marriage to a pediatrician I knew any potential future divorce cost would place me at less risk. I sent a letter of introduction in August 1990. She called four months later, in December, after I had completely forgotten about it. By then my business had become even more financially miserable, as the Taxi and Limousine Commission lifted half of my medallions because I did not have the money to pay the arrears of the Workman's Comp policies instituted by the State "18 months retroactive," with the drain of my divorce dragging on. I paid legal bills for both sides. The judge had ruled that if my trial resulted in upholding the prenuptual the expenses that I paid her lawyer would offset what I would owe in the prenuptial agreement to the soon to become ex-wife.

Just after I got my medallions back on the road after the financial trauma imposed by the New York City and State new Workman's Comp requirement for contracted cab drivers in New York City, I finally met "Cute pediatrician, 31." This took place in December 1990, four months after I sent the letter of introduction, when she called me.

After we finally met, we dated. She looked perfect on paper. We both wanted children. We both liked eating out and going to movies.

We toured most all of China and Tibet on our honeymoon. We got pregnant right away. Two months after the birth of our first child, a boy, the new Workman's Comp policies claimed the last life of my shrinking cab business which by that time made no money because of the new government expenses for Workman's Comp for cab drivers contracted by the shift and only one fare raise in nine years. I still had my garage and a spare cab to make money. I found myself forced to borrow money from my new wife to keep my fleet in equilibrium. She required letters of percentage ownership, a strategy which helped her in the future, which you will read about in the upcoming chapters.

My new wife, Ayse (pronounced [ai-shuh], required me to help pay for (1) an investment apartment next door which she owned, (2) a $1,000,000 life insurance policy for her, and (3) a physical health and mental health disability insurance policy for her for $500,000, no longer available for issuing new policies. The insurance company stopped issuing new policies because, by report, too many doctors had gotten colleagues to certify that they had physical health or mental health issues, allowing them to retire with $500,000.

I knew we had a problem when she asked me if I would collect the million dollars from the life insurance policy and give her the money if she had some med school friends in Turkey certify that she had died. I said no.

She said she planned to collect the half million dollar disability insurance policy at some point.

I try not to seem too harsh on her as we have two children together, as we will for life. The story just keeps getting more interesting. After she became pregnant with our second child, she became more and more mean.

First son, Eric
Only daughter, Lara

The one meeting
of the countess
and the Patron
Saint of Grifters
at the mansion in
Greenwich, CT.

Wedding Day
August 8, 1991

Daughter Lara

Daughter Lara,
student at Tulane

Lobby in apartment
on W- 72nd St at
Broadway where she
met Hamdi Ulukaya

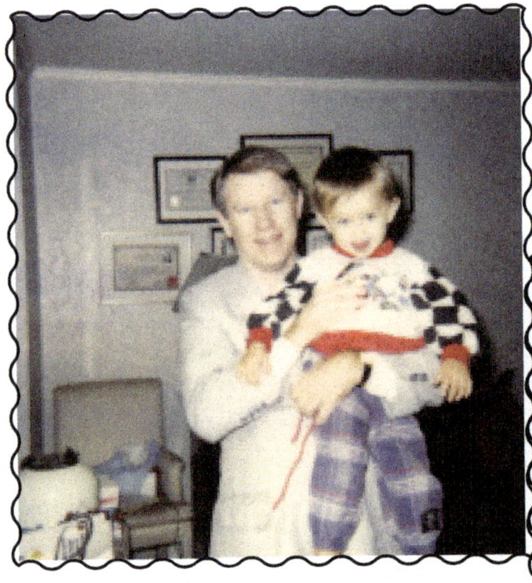

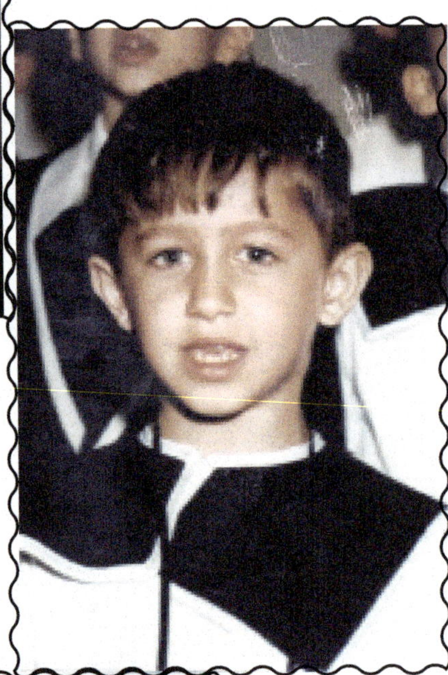

Third marriage
Patron Saint
of Grifters and
first child, Eric

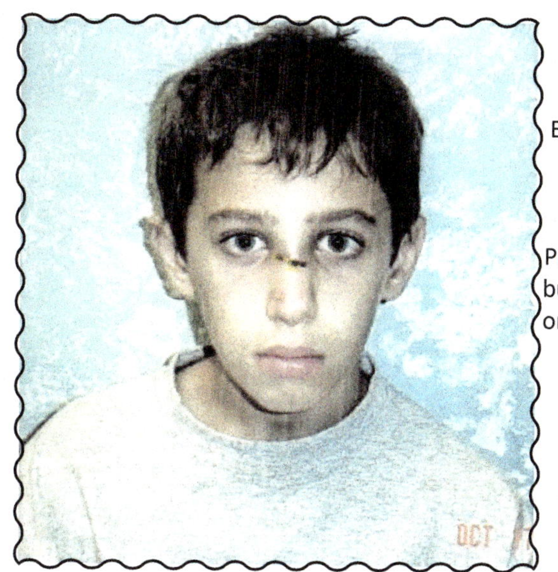

Eric Cruey, my first child whose mother changed his name to Giray after she stole him. He is the boy who sued Calhoun Prep School eight years later for bullying. At this time he was still on the international missing list.

Eric at the resort that collapsed in an earthquake the following summer

Chapter 28
A Brief History Lesson of the New York City Taxi Medallion Industry

Where do I go to get my taxi fleet back since the City and State of New York, under Governor Mario Cuomo, stole it from me?

This happened before the 1992 election when Mario Cuomo had thought of running for president, but his ongoing massive increases in welfare programs put the budget of the State of New York under water. To make up the shortfall, he and the legislature came up with a plan to charge each New York City taxi medallion $2,500 per year for a previously non-existent Workman's Compensation policy, to pay to a company owned by the State of New York. The amount due went from zero to $2,500. This fee applied to no other taxis in the State. We taxi fleet owners could not move to New Jersey as the New York Stock Exchange threatened to do when presented with high proposed fees by New York State.

Even the Taxi and Limousine Commission seemed aghast when the State of New Yok forced the City to pull the medallions from the owners for these worthless policies, never before needed since automobiles began driving in New York 90 years before.

Even my taxi broker, who owned several taxi medallions himself, said, "From now on we will be working for the City and State of New York, not really for ourselves, as all of our spare/meager profit will go to pay the City and State Government."

Because of that, I laugh when I see the national TV commercials inviting businesses to relocate to New York State, claiming that they have lower taxes than a few years ago.

All of the other Workman's Compensation companies had

abandoned New York State because of ghetto juries awarding high claims for minor accidents. As a result, the State of New York ended up owning the only Workman's Comp insurance company in the State at that time. Before he could run for president, the governor needed a massive infusion of cash to balance the budget. He never did run because the State did not raise enough money to balance the budget.

I no longer feel angry at Mario Cuomo for destroying my taxi fleet because I saved the next 25 years of my life not managing my 51 taxicabs. The future of the New York City taxi business became bleak after New York City released onto the market approximately a couple thousand new taxi medallions for up to/or more than $1,000,000 each, keeping the money for the City coffers to pay for more welfare programs.

The City also shrank the available road space in Manhattan for motor vehicles by putting in bike lanes so that cab drivers could not make much money. The last straw came from the competition from Uber entering the taxi marketplace, truly putting the taxi fleet owners under water.

By borrowing money against the medallions, the fleet owners protected the value of the medallions against frivolous judgments made by runaway ghetto juries. Having medallions encumbered by loans shielded the medallions against these artificially high judgments.

I once took a cab from downtown Bombay (Mumbai) where the cabs waited in a four-mile long line waiting for a fare. This happens when you have corrupt city administrators selling permits indiscriminately.

It feels good to vent.

Chapter 29
The Start of Chobani and the Later Yogurt Wars/ Genghis Khan

Bottom line, when the City and State of New York ruined my taxi fleet investment ability to turn a profit, I sold and moved to Las Vegas. It turned out for the best because those that stayed in the fleet business 20 more years found themselves under water because of Uber. I applied my fleet management and assembly skills to start up and do well in the trucking and oil business. I sold just before the oil business crashed.

I still wish I had used my GI Bill credits to start the first chain of McDonald's in New York City.

I apologize to the reader if some of the following events seem hard to follow but I myself did not learn of the true sequence until 14 years later.

In my four-year marriage to Ayşe, we had turmoil in our troubled relationship, with two children under the age of three, and questionable whether we would stay together. We talked about the budget. At that point, all my spare cash went to her and her pathetic budget. We decided that she would sell the two apartments at the Princeton House at 95th and Broadway, including the two bedroom, two bath model apartment where we lived on the second floor, and the adjoining one-bedroom apartment next to it. We had at one time considered joining the two apartments to have more living space. We had purchased the second apartment next to our primary apartment as an investment. Our high fixed payments contributed to the breakdown of our relationship. The fixed payments included:

- the two apartment mortgages

- the payment for the $1,000,000 life insurance policy on her life
- the $500,000 disability insurance policy on her – remember this $500,000 figure as it will come up later in this book

As a Turkish-American pediatrician in New York City she had many Turkish patients. Through them, she had a friend who had an inexpensive rent-controlled apartment to sublet to her/us if we stayed together, in a nice and vastly cheaper apartment on 72nd Street just east of Broadway. Our budget would find huge, instant relief. I helped her move into the new, almost as nice, and infinitely cheaper apartment. She had agreed that I would pay less money to her with the now reduced expenses.

We went through with the divorce. As part of the divorce, she wanted full custody of our two children. I agreed to this because she would find it difficult to go back and forth to Turkey every summer if she had to get a permission slip from me each time. We worked out iron-tight visitation dates through the Manhattan Family Court which she eventually completely ignored. We had agreed that I would have informal unlimited visitation rights. I had obtained full legal visitation rights, but when she could not get me back after trying everything in the book to do so, she promptly prevented the children from seeing me, forever. She stated: "We come as a package."

In a fire started by a spark from a welding torch on a cab on the top of the lift in my garage, the car turned into an inferno, burning a hole in the top of the roof and melting the steel beams that supported the roof. Once the beams melted, you could not repair the building, but would have to build a completely new building.

My garage at 542 West 53rd Street, New York, New York, burned down on June 3, 1996, without fire insurance because the City of New York owned the building. For $250,000 I had bought the stock that had the rights to the lease for the property from the owner of the lifetime lease issued by the New York City Real Estate Department. This all formed part of the Times Square Redevelopment Corporation

Karen and I married November 10, 1996, coinciding with my parents' 50th wedding anniversary. We moved out west after Karen completed her Child and Adolescent Psychiatry Residency Training Program at the end of June 1997.

In September 1997 Ayşe called to ask if I would consider ever coming back. I said no. Note this date for the future.

Unbeknown to me for the next 14 years when I finally pieced together the information, she married her new husband in September 1997.

Fourteen years later I learned that she had befriended a man from Eastern Turkey, 12 years her junior, selling fruit at his fruit stand at 72nd and Broadway, near where she now lived. Fourteen years later she told me this story, that he had entered the United States with a Student Visa to go to SUNY Albany, somehow he never went there, and his visa expired.

I learned, years later after she stopped my visits with my children after the summer of 1998 when I saw them for the last time, that she had already married her new husband. I went to visit my 3 ½ year old daughter and my just seven year old son at a seaside town on the Marmursk Sea in Turkey, where the family owned a vacation home in an elite compound a mile or two out of town, 70 miles from Istanbul, the family's year-round home. I took a hotel room in town, where I stayed.

The family compound collapsed in the deadly Turkish earthquake of 1999. This earthquake set in motion her elaborate plot to hide the children from me for the next 14 years.

Implementation of the plot began when her sister told me that Ayşe and the children had moved to Izmir, Turkey, a town in the south of the country, following the damage of the earthquake, and that they would not return to New York.

After paying Child Support payments into the New York State Child Support Collection Unit for many years, I learned that the money went unclaimed. I could not find Ayse or my children. The Family Court judge could not find her. I had no reason to believe that she had remained in New York. The Family Court Judge said that he would give me full custody if he could find her. We later found that she had used an assumed name that helped her hide from creditors.

The New York State Child Support Collections unit refunded me $26,000 of unclaimed child support. They told me that this had never happened previously.

In 2008, the office assistant at my wife's psychiatry office overheard me talking about my missing children. She asked for the children's names and for the mother's maiden name. She googled the name "Eric Giray" and it came up as a boy playing on an after-school soccer team in lower Manhattan. This gave me the first indication that the children lived in America.

Even after finding out that they lived in New York City it took lawyers and court orders to drag Ayşe into court. My lawyer set up a court date to meet my daughter Lara. My son Eric had gone to China to study Chinese during his senior year in high school, and could not attend the court date.

I received the most unusual phone call of my life in 2012, on the Friday after Thanksgiving. An attorney representing Hamdi Ulukaya, Ayşe's former husband, called my office in Las Vegas. I never knew that she had remarried and divorced again. I had never before heard of Hamdi Ulukaya, Chobani Yogurt, or the Yogurt Wars prior to this phone call. The attorney who called me at my office told me that Ayşe Giray had initiated a lawsuit for just over a half billion dollars for 53% control of the stock of Chobani Yogurt. I asked him, "Don't you mean a half a million dollars?" He responded, "No, a half a billion dollars." I almost fell off my chair. I told the attorney that Ayşe had a history of negative behaviors. He responded that they knew about her negative behaviors. I told him that I would have to side with Ayşe in this case as she had my children with her, and if she won in a lawsuit it would benefit my children. He never called again.

I had not known that Ayşe had an additional marriage. It turned out that when I visited the family vacation home for the two-hour sessions in July of 1998, she had already married her new husband but she did not wear a wedding ring or tell me that she had married.

I felt very surprised to hear of the half billion dollar lawsuit for 53% control of Chobani Yogurt as I knew that she had ripped off New York all those years living in subsidized housing as well as receiving SSD payments from the U. S. Government, all the while hiding my children.

When reviewing the merits of continuing SSI or SSD payments and other benefits to individuals, the U. S. Government may want to adjust its practice of due diligence in view of the previously mentioned case.

By the phone call from the attorney on behalf of Mr. Ulukaya, it all pieced together. Ayşe had gotten declared mentally disabled which allowed her to cash in her $500,000.00 disability policy for which I had helped her pay premiums. It seems that she took this half million dollars and through various dealings, funded the start of Chobani Yogurt. Subsequently I called Ayşe and she gave me the interval history which included the information that 25-year-old Hamdi Ulukaya started out as a fruit vendor at 72nd and Broadway, where she met him, near the apartment into which I had helped her move with the children.

Many people may remember the case of the private school boy who sued for bullying both an ex-student and Calhoun School, the top prep school in Manhattan where JFK Jr. attended, for $1.5 million eight years after the event, where the other student pushed him down bleacher stairs. Under his mother's guidance and his changed surname to that of his mother, this lawsuit came from my son, on the U. S. State Department's Missing Children List at the time.

She cashed in her disability insurance policy based on a mental health complaint for a half million dollars and bankrolled Hamdi's start of Chobani Yogurt. I paid part of the premiums on that policy.

My new wife Karen and I went on to have twin boys out in Las Vegas and a great life. I went into the oil, biodiesel, and trucking business.

In the spring of 2013, I received the second most interesting / bizarre phone call of my life. A representative for a London finance business called me at my office to get background information from me regarding their possible loan of $800,000,000 to Chobani, in view of Ayşe's 53% open court case for control of Chobani. I told them that she had said to me that she did not want control of it, but took that position as posturing.

Three weeks later Hamdi and Chobani got the $ 800 million, so he did not have to go public and kept the freedom to expand. On a visit to Southern California, I saw the signs in McDonald's for the Chobani yogurt parfaits and smoothies. I hear Chobani has done quite well.

Wikipedia called the Giray name second only to the Ottomans in Turkey. The same Wikipedia article stated that the Girays descended from Genghis Khan. My ex apparently now holds a significant amount of Chobani stock and likely lives in or near Palm Beach, FL, as I recommended to her. The Genghis Khan bloodline has finally made it to Palm Beach, in two of my four children. As a businessman I don't hold anything against her in getting in this position. I only regret that she hid my children from me.

With all said and done, I had only a few bad years in an otherwise exciting and enjoyable life.

In the late 1950's my great aunt, Theresa Lange Schlereth, an immigrant from Germany, whose parents used to own newspapers, visited us in Pompano Beach, FL, from time to time. She would have us drive her to Palm Beach to see where the really rich lived. I feel sure that it would make her happy to know that her great, great nephew and niece finally made it.

Although a Protestant, I consider myself the patron saint of paperboys, teenage motorcyclists in Europe, Vietnam era U. S. Army draftees, and cab drivers. Starting as a 23-year-old stock broker/investment banker at Shields & Company at 44 Wall Street, I used my Veteran's benefits to buy a taxicab. I drove my cab at night, and turned my earnings into a fleet of 51 taxicabs. Future Hot Shots, beat that!

Also, I once married the patron saint of grifters. She, in turn, later married the Ultimate Hot Shot. He became one of the few owners in the last twenty or thirty years of a multi-billion dollar company not in the high tech industry. Of current interest, Hamdi Ulukaya has linked up with Bill Gates and Warren Buffett to start a refugee charity with his company's billions. The initial financing of the startup of Chobani Yogurt came from a loan from his ex-wife obtained from her disability insurance settlement from a policy for which I paid a large part.

Whenever my wife, Karen, and I see Chobani Yogurt advertised or for sale in a shop, we salute. I wonder if Chobani Yogurt would have come into existence without the roles that we all played. It seems impossible to me.

Chapter 30
Bully Lawsuit – Yale – State Department

The headlines in the New York newspapers gave extensive coverage to the bullying lawsuit by a former student against another student and his former, prestigious private school.

Many people may remember the case of the private school boy who sued for bullying both an ex-student and Calhoun School, the top prep school in Manhattan where JFK Jr. attended, for $1.5 million eight years after the event, where the other student pushed him down bleacher stairs. Under his mother's guidance and his changed surname to that of his mother, this lawsuit came from my son, Erik, on the missing children's list at the time.

The Manhattan Family Court judge told me that he would give full custody to me, the children's father, of both Erik and his sister Lara, if only we could find them. We did not find them until years later after they had gotten too old for court-ordered visitation.

Because of rumors that my son, Eric, had gone to Yale and since I hadn't seen him since he was seven, I went to Yale to the Provost office where they said they couldn't release information. I informed the Yale staff member that he had gotten stolen by his mother who violated court ordered visitation rights, a seven year felony in New York, but not enforced in this case. I have wondered if my children suffer from a form of the Stockholm syndrome, identifying with their captor.

The provost of Yale came out, made an exception, and told me that my son does not attend Yale. It turned out that he got accepted to Yale with an offer of a one-year scholarship. Instead of going to Yale, he went to another college that offered him a four year scholarship. It seems hard to believe that some people actually turn down Yale. He had only to call me for the money but his mother prevented it. She put more priority on keeping him hidden than sending her only son to Yale.

One summer he even interned at the State Department, possibly the only person to do so while on the State Department's Missing Children list.

Chapter 31
Enter the Love of My Life
(And more assorted Hot Shot travel stories)

My old girlfriend, Karen, came back into my life during her psychiatry residency training here in New York City, always the nicest person I had known, a great cook, and very attractive. I had my two children, finally. Where do I go to get a nice wife?

In late June 1997 after Karen finished her residency in child and adolescent psychiatry we took off for a grand tour of North America, driving all the way to the far reaches of Alaska and back.

During her first locum tenens assignment — which means to take the place of another person temporarily, and in healthcare, it means physicians who fill in for other physicians on an interim basis — in Longview, Washington, every weekend for 10 weeks we went in a different direction to see the sights. We saw Mount Saint Helens where the volcano erupted in 1980 in Washington State, the Petrified Forest, Crater Lake, the rain forest of Olympia, Washington, and many of the places that Lewis and Clark camped. As we drove, we listened to a many-volume Book on Tape telling about their experiences.

In mid-October we stayed in the heart of San Francisco for two weeks, then to Phoenix which still had blistering hot temperatures for more locum tenens work that fall.

After spending a very pleasant Christmas with my parents in Arkansas, we drove to Miami where we caught a flight to Ecuador, first to Guayaquil and then to the Galapagos for a cruise around the Galapagos Island. In a park we saw Harriet, the Galapagos tortoise, alive and well at the age of 168 years at the time of our visit, collected by Charles Darwin in 1835. When snorkeling in the Galapagos we saw large sharks swimming underneath us. We saw marine iguanas feeding on underwater algae.

We flew back to Miami. My wife flew to Las Vegas to start another locum tenens job. I drove the SUV to New York to pick up the contents of our storage. I drove to Las Vegas arriving January 30, 1998.

My credentials included having a Bachelor of Science degree from USC, majoring in Finance, Marketing, and Management. They considered USC as the best undergraduate business school west of Wharton in Philadelphia.

My first activities in Las Vegas included buying five acres of land. Having lived in Manhattan for so many years, we felt proud to own land. We sold the land for a nice profit six years later, two years before the real estate crash. We made more profit and had less risk than building homes to sell on the land.

In June of 1998 we had in-vitro fertilization, resulting in the birth of our twin boys on January 8, 1999.

Other business ventures included an offshoot of the biodiesel business where I owned many large tanker and pump trucks. We built up accounts from San Francisco to Dallas and from Wyoming to San Diego, for the collection of yellow grease (used French fry oil) for biodiesel and other uses. I sold out in the early fall of 2014 before the price of oil crashed.

Now I do occasional venture capital deals in the energy beverage field as well as world-wide Internet scuba diving information. Some years ago, we put together an extensive medical information website, www.us-md.com, ranked by Google at the time as 19th best in the world, next to Web M.D.

A few years ago my wife received an invitation to a World Health Organization psychiatric congress in Havana, Cuba, through the American Academy of Child and Adolescent Psychiatry. Naturally I wanted to attend. I applied for and received permission from the U. S. State Department to travel to this highly restricted destination as "clinical coordinator." When we arrived in Havana, we met one of the other U.S. attendees, the former president of the American Academy of Child & Adolescent Psychiatry who wondered how I got a visa as her husband could not get one. I simply said that I applied as the clinic coordinator, and obtained the visa. I attended the psychiatric congress for three days before renting a car for cash. I traveled all over Cuba for four days, possibly the only American to do so at that time.

For our honeymoon in 1997, we traveled throughout the Caribbean and went scuba diving at many beautiful islands. When we went to Haiti, we mistakenly thought that we could drive around the island. Because of the deep potholes in the roads we did not make six miles before we had to turn back. We found the environment very dangerous. We stayed at the Hotel Montana where all the Americans stayed, subsequently leveled by the earthquake some years later.

We have taken many memorable trips throughout the world in our 20 years of marriage. We began one trip going from Los Angeles to Sydney, Australia, just before the 2000 Summer Olympics in Sydney. We stayed in a hotel overlooking the Sydney Opera House which had a fabulous light show of colorful changing lights throughout the night. We toured the Olympic area before catching our flight to Hong Kong where we spent a day or two shopping and sightseeing before going to Vietnam.

When we landed in Hanoi in North Vietnam we felt interested to see water buffalo working the rice paddy across the street from the airport. We had a hotel near the Hanoi Hilton where John McCain stayed during his years as prisoner of war. We visited central and South Vietnam also, including Haiphong Harbor, Hue, Ho Chi Minh City (formerly Saigon), Danang, Khe Sanh, and many others. We went scuba diving along the central, South Vietnamese coast.

We went on to Cambodia by land, dangerous at the border, and not recommended for tourists, we realized. It had the worst roads that we had seen since Haiti. In Cambodia we visited the dramatic ruins at Angor Wat. From there we went to Bangkok where we stayed at the world-famous Mandarin Oriental Hotel, to Kuala Lumpur in Malaysia, and finally to Singapore with the busiest harbor in the world, from where we went home.

When on the maiden Christmas cruise in the Caribbean for the new Queen Mary 2 with Karen, our twin boys, and my parents, we learned of the catastrophic tsunami in Indonesia that occurred on December 26, 2004. Karen received an invitation to speak at a Continuing Medical Education Conference in Bangkok the next summer. She, the six-year-old twins, and I went on the trip. The boys and I visited my old Army base in Thailand, Camp Friendship. Because of the tsunami which had affected Thailand, she spoke on posttraumatic stress disorder at the conference. From the conference we went on a tour of Thailand with the physician attendees of the conference and their families. We went to Pattaya Beach where we had had R & R for the combat troops from Vietnam.

When I served at Camp Friendship in 1968, the colonel to whom I reported, offered me my own post, the R & R center at Pattaya Beach, if I would extend my service in the U. S. Army by one year. I declined.

In Chiang Mai, founded in the late 13th century, located near the Golden Triangle where Thailand, Laos, and Myanmar (the former Burma) meet, we rode on elephants.

Out of Chiang Mai we went to the village of the long-necked people, where women and girls wrap brass-appearing coils around their necks that create the long-necked effect. The long-necked people felt fascinated to see our blond-hair twins and asked to touch their hair.

At the Golden Triangle we rode in a small boat across the muddy Mekong River into Laos for a short visit.

We flew from Chiang Mai back to Bangkok, and then to Japan. After touring southern Japan, we took the bullet train north to take a Russian ship to Vladivostok, an important Russian seaport and formerly of military significance. Wonderful Intourist guides, articulate in English, got us onto the Trans-Siberian Railroad and met us at every stop. We saw Lake Baikal, the largest freshwater lake in the world, with ice six feet deep in the winter, used in past as a winter highway. Before going on to Moscow, we saw Kursk and Ekaterinburg, where the Czar and his family died in 1919.

After touring the national museums, at the Bolshoi Theater we attended a magnificent performance of The Nutcracker performed by the Bolshoi Ballet.

While in Moscow, on prior arrangement by the contracting law firm Karen interviewed a woman who had initiated a law suit against a large organization for injuries suffered while in the United States but who could not obtain a visa to return to the USA for the court appearances.

We went on to Minsk and then to Kiev where we no longer had the Intourist agent to help us along the way. In Kiev on our own, we went to the train station and asked for four tickets to Krakow, Poland. We rode until late at night on the train, got a hotel, got up and walked around, and finally went to a travel agency. While there getting further bookings, I asked where the Pope had lived as a child. They could not understand our question. Only then did we discover that we had gone to Kharkov, in the Ukraine near the Russian border, instead of Krakow in Poland. Kharkov saw many great tank battles in World War II. More recently it saw new, military conflict as the eastern Ukraine sought to pull out of the orbit of Russia.

We returned to Kiev where Karen took a plane to Berlin. The boys and I travelled on by train to Krakow, Poland, and then to Berlin where I hired the last of the six lawyers needed to try to find my missing children in Germany, in view of the repeated misdirection received from the Giray family.

We really enjoyed the trip, taking 51 days to go around the world, and my third trip around the world.

For three weeks starting in December 2005, Karen and I went on a three-week trip to Australia, where we left winter in the Northern Hemisphere and went into summer in the Southern Hemisphere. After fourteen hours on a very pleasant flight on Qantas from Los Angeles to Sydney, we had to run about half a mile through the terminal to catch our connecting flight to Ayer's Rock in the Australian Outback. They held the flight for us, as they had no other flight for 24 hours.

In the Outback we saw one of the most impressive shows of our lives. We took a shuttle to a remote area where they had a cocktail party followed by an excellent dinner for about 100 people. You could hear an audible gasp from the guests when all the lights went out after the meal, revealing the brilliant Southern Constellations in the cloudless night sky. An astronomer using a laser pointer described the details of the constellations, and their seasonal changes.

Following two days in the Outback, we flew back to Sydney where we joined the Australian Pacific Tours (APT) group that took us on a coach, not a bus, with a driver and a tour guide, up the east coast of Australia. We recommend this tour. We stayed at a different exotic resort every night or two. We went scuba diving on the Great Barrier Reef in three places. The trip included a day of white water rafting. We went through the tropical forests of northern Australia. The tour ended in Cairns, on the Coral Sea. We flew from Cairns to Melbourne, where we looked in on the Australian Tennis Open in January 2006 as well as a world class poker tournament in Melbourne, by the beautiful River Walk. From Melbourne we flew to Hobart in southern Tasmania. We happened to arrive in Hobart at the conclusion of the Fastnet sailboat race from Sydney, and saw the boats and their crews at dock. In a rental car we drove around the island of Tasmania.

In 2012, I took the twins on a tour of Scandinavia and came down through Estonia, Latvia, and Lithuania. We went through Poland where we visited the Auschwitz concentration camp.

Since then we have crossed the Atlantic four years in a row on the Queen Mary 2 to travel Europe for the summer with our teenaged twin boys. This coming Christmas will mark our third Christmas cruise on the Queen Mary. On one of those trips we took a house in the London suburbs for three weeks during the London summer Olympic Games. Karen and I had such a good time at the Athens Olympics eight years earlier, we had to return for the London Olympics.

For the summer of 2016 progress report, my wife and I together with our 17-year-old twin boys traveled to England on a seven-day cruise from New York City across the Atlantic for the fourth year in a row on the beautiful ocean liner, the Queen Mary 2. We sailed away on 7/06/2016 and arrived at Southampton in southern England on 7/13/2016. We went to the airport and immediately flew to Nice, France.

In keeping with my Forrest Gump life format, we managed to dodge the terrorist truck driver who attacked and killed 85 men, women, and children who had watched the Bastille Day fireworks by the beach on July 14th in Nice. From our hotel a mile or two away, sirens from the police cars and ambulances woke us up throughout the night. We had driven to St. Tropez for the day and felt too tired to do anything other than have dinner and go to bed instead of going to see the fireworks with everyone else. After the terrorist attack in Nice, the car rental prices dropped 60%. At the airport car rental hub in Nice, they had acres of available rental cars available. They had the especially low price available for those who did not have a reservation. Note to Hot Shots: while traveling, do not make reservations if you want the best prices.

In Cannes, our boys had a great time in a secure compound on the beach for two weeks at the French language school and party atmosphere after school, and a great place for Hot Shots to send their teenagers.

Later we went on to travel to Toulon, France, where Napoleon got his military start. We went to Marseille, the largest port in the Mediterranean, and saw all the ships including cruise ships as well as commercial vessels of various kinds. We visited Avignon on the Rhone River in France where the Catholic Church moved the Papacy from Rome between 1309 and 1376.

We went on to Andorra, a beautiful ski resort in the Pyrenees Mountains, nestled between Spain and France.

Lourdes, Frances, became famous after Bernadette Soubirous, who later became a saint, had on 18 different occasions a vision or visitation from the Virgin Mary. In addition to the famous grotto and many pilgrims, we saw homes for retired nuns and homes for retired priests.

After Lourdes, we went to Biarritz, a first-class resort in France on the Atlantic Ocean, with great surfing and poker playing at the casino.

In the Basque section of northern Spain, we visited Bilbao, known for its art museums including the world famous Guggenheim Museum which we visited. In northern Spain we also saw the cathedral of El Camino de Santiago de Compostela, the destination for pilgrims who walk hundreds of miles to pay their respects. We met one couple in their 20's who had walked 600 miles in their pilgrimage.

In Porto, Portugal, the home of port wine, we drove through and spent the night on our way to Fatima, another Catholic spiritual town.

In Fatima, the Blessed Virgin Mary appeared six times to three shepherd children between May 13 and October 13, 1917. The Holy Mother urged them to say the rosary daily and to pray for world peace. We saw thousands of pilgrims from all over the world at Fatima.

On Portugal's Atlantic Coast, Nazra, a world class summer resort, has the highest surf in the world in the winter, with international surfing competitions held there. In July, we had fun watching various sized motor boats that would pull the surfers the long distance out in the water to reach the surfable waves.

On the beach side of Lisbon, Estoril, Portugal, over the centuries became the home of many of Europe's deposed royalty. The casino in Estoril has good poker games. By the way, if you Hot Shots ever want to see some of these deposed royals in one place, go to the Red Cross Ball in Monaco, founded by Princess Grace, held on the first Friday every August. I can attest to this as I went to the ball several times in the past, dancing on the dance floor next to Princess Grace's kids.

Salamanca, Spain, a day's drive from Estoril, has a fabulous cathedral, worthy of a trip to Salamanca to view it. The cathedral, built in 1102, underwent renovation in 1992 with addition of a small carved replica of a modern astronaut on an exterior wall.

The saying, "The rain in Spain stays mainly in the plain," made famous in the musical My Fair Lady, might have originated from observation of the exotic plains in the central northern parts of Spain. I admit to singing the tune repeatedly while driving through the area and observing the plains.

We saw the famous town of Burgos, home of El Cid, Spanish hero. In Burgos they discovered human remains 1,000,000 years old, (+/-) 100,000 years. Because of that, they built the world-famous Early Man Museum to house findings of early man from all over the world. The museum contains the 3 ½ million year old skull of Lucy, the earliest known full skull of Homo erectus, found in Northern Kenya. Lucy received her name by the finders of her skeleton because the Beatle's song, Lucy in the Sky with Diamonds, came on the radio at the campsite the night of the find, by report.

We continued on to Pamplona, famous for the Running of the Bulls every year on July 7th , made famous by Earnest Hemingway's book, "For Whom the Bell Tolls."

Barcelona, a several-hour drive and one of my favorite cities in Europe along with London, Paris, Venice, Cannes, St. Tropez, and Zurich, has great beaches, nightclubs, and shopping. They have a great poker tournament at the casino the second half of every August. Barcelona has several beautiful cathedrals including the dramatic, still unfinished Sagrada Familia (Sacred Family) Cathedral, where work began March 19, 1882.

In Monaco for a day pass at the principal beach club, it costs $200 per person.

Portofino, a picturesque town just past Genoa on the Mediterranean, may have become a destination for yachting trips in part because of the limited parking availability for cars.

The city of Pisa in Tuscany, originally an important seaport and city state on the coast of the Ligurian Sea until silt in the River Arno interfered, received its name in 600 B.C. from a Greek word meaning "marshy land." We saw the amazing Leaning Tower of Pisa, also known as the Torre Pendente di Pisa, built in the Romanesque style of architecture between 1173 and 1399, in the Campo dei Miracoli (Field of Miracles) together with Il Duomo (the Cathedral) and the Baptistery, where the baptism of Galileo took place in 1505. While the Leaning Tower had an original height of 60 meters, more recently it measured 56.67 meters on the highest side and 55.86 meters on the lowest side, with 0.81 meters in height difference between the highest and the lowest sides. Due to water under the ground, by report the original project engineer, Bonanno Pisano could place the tower's foundation only about five to ten feet under the ground, a shallow foundation for a 60 meter building that would come to weigh an estimated 14, 500 metric tons.

By way of Siena, we traveled through Tuscany to Florence. We visited many amazing locations. We saw and toured the famous Ponte Vecchio, the covered bridge filled with vendors' shops and businesses over the River Arno. We read that the term bankruptcy originated on the Ponte Vecchio. When a money changer could not pay his debts, soldiers came and broke ("rotto") his table ("banco") resulting in "bancorotto," making it impossible for him to conduct business further. The Uffizi Gallery, originally called the Uffizi Palace and built to house government offices or "uffizi," provided a space for the Medici family that ruled Florence at one time and became patrons of many important artists, to hang the paintings that they owned on the walls. The Uffizi Gallery houses works of Giotto, Botticelli, Leonardo da Vinci, and Michelangelo among others. We viewed the Gucci Museum with its famous clothing, shoes, purses, and other designs over the years.

Out of Florence on the road to Venice, we passed through the town of Modena which has two car factory/museums with tours. One day take the tour of the Lamborghini factory and museum for $300 per person for the day. The next day take the Ferrari factory and museum tour for $300 per person for the day.

After a day in Venice, we drove four hours to Slovenia and on through Zagreb, Croatia, on our way to Sarajevo, Bosnia, once the home of the Winter Olympics and the location of the assassination of the Archduke

Ferdinand, the flashpoint triggering the start of World War I in early August 1914. We headed south to Mostar, Bosnia, the city in Europe with the hottest temperatures. We saw the famous Bridge of Mostar from a distance. It interested us to see bullet holes from war combat 20 years ago in the higher parts of buildings all along the road. In the ancient walled city and port town of Dubrovnik, a popular European tourist destination, we saw many cruise ships in the harbor.

The country of Montenegro has many beach front towns also frequented by cruise ships. In Albania we felt surprised to see many Mercedes cars driven on the road. When I asked about how so many people could afford to drive Mercedes vehicles, the person responded jokingly that possibly the owners belonged to the Mafia.

After an eight-hour trip from the Albania border, we spent a day in Athens where we toured the modern Olympic stadium as well as the ancient marble Olympic stadium in addition to the Parthenon (Acropolis). The next morning we drove to the port city of Piraeus where I had first visited 50 years ago. We took advantage of the super highways to drive quickly to Macedonia where we stayed in capital city at the Alexander the Great Palace Hotel.

The next day in the new country of Kosovo, we saw the Bill Klinton Boulevard. We found out that you cannot legally enter Serbia from Kosovo. We had to go back to Macedonia to enter Serbia, where we drove around and went on our way to Romania. When we got to Romania, we realized that if we drove an entire day to the east we could see the Transylvania Mountains and Count Dracula's castle, so we did that, a day there and a day back.

When we got to Budapest, Hungary, we found the city full of youthful people enjoying a weeklong concert that attracted youth from all over Europe. We ate delicious Hungarian goulash in one of the restaurants, and went on to Vienna where we spent the night.

Vienna looked as beautiful as I always remembered it. In the winter they have Viennese balls, affordable and spectacular, that Hot Shots should consider attending. I never saw so many beautiful women in one place before with the possible exception of the Ford Modeling Agency Christmas Party in New York and certain sororities at the University of Southern California.

After walking around the park and the shopping district, we went by the old casino where I played poker years before.

At the next stop, Salzburg, the city has the world-famous music festival in the last six weeks of the summer every year. We ended up in Innsbruck, a beautiful city and a central focus point of Austrian snow skiing.

From Innsbruck we went on to Zurich, Switzerland, where we toured the world-famous Museum of the Renaissance. We had a great time in Zurich, a beautiful and fun town. From Zurich we went to Basel, 50 miles to the north from where my grandfather grew up, where we toured more museums. We saw a fabulous 20's, 30's, and 40's car show on the street in a really fancy part of town, including Duzenbergs, Morgans, and others. On the QT, we learned that German Swiss look down on Germans because of the way they disgraced themselves in World War II, even now refusing to intermarry with them.

The next day we drove to Lucerne, a beautiful city on a river, and drove on a winding road up to the ski resort town of Zermatt in the Alps, at the foot of the Matterhorn Mountain, the tallest peak in Europe. We went skiing on August 16th taking multiple arrays of ski lifts to get to the top. We would expect Hot Shots to make it a goal to take their teenagers there in the summer.

We drove back down winding roads in the Swiss Alps, with many long tunnels, into the Italian Alps and into Milan, Italy, the world fashion destination, and famous for the cathedral Il Domo and La Scala, the Milan Opera House. Hot Shots should consider coming during opera season to attend a performance in this breathtaking building. After two days in Milan, we drove to Villa D'Este, the most beautiful hotel in the world on Lake Como.

We spent the night in Bellagio, known for its world famous beauty and after which they named the Hotel Bellagio in Las Vegas. The next day we stopped in Verona and saw the 1,900 year old outdoor opera theater, still in use to this day, and other Roman architecture throughout the city. Remember Shakespeare's play, "Two Gentlemen from Verona"?

From Lake Como to Venice took all day. We dropped off our rental car, giving us two additional days to tour the city in addition to our one day in Venice earlier, enabling us to see all of Venice. You need to walk to Venice in three different directions, each day setting off in a different way, with each more exotic than the next.

Hot Shots: when I first traveled all over Europe and the Middle East in 1966 I saw four times fewer vehicles on the road. They had very few super highways. You could easily find your way around on two-lane roads to everywhere. Now, all the signs point you to "Pay Toll" superhighways where you see very little of the countryside. The signs out of all towns lack detail. This trip has convinced me to use cell phone GPS navigation to go virtually everywhere.

From Venice we flew to Istanbul in preparation to flying to Houston. In the day we spent in Istanbul I took the boys to the Blue Mosque, the Topkapi Palace, the home of the sultans, and the Hagia Sofia completed as a cathedral in 637, then the tallest building in the planet, and which became a mosque after the Ottoman Empire took over the city in 1453.

Established on the site of the ancient Greek colony of Byzantium, the city became Constantinople in the year 330 AD and the capital of the Eastern Roman Empire with the Roman emperor Constantine I, five years after Constantine made Christianity the Roman Empire's official religion, per history.com, once "an obscure Jewish sect." The Western half of the Roman Empire collapsed in 476. Constantinople became the center of the Byzantine Empire.

In the year 1453 the Ottoman Empire overran Constantinople and changed the name from Constantinople to Istanbul.

I see life as good. I have 35 good years left. As I dedicate the rest of my life to as many healthy, safe adventures as possible, another Great Hot Shot adventure book will emerge.

Now I do venture capital deals taking ten percent of future worldwide companies. We owned 100% of US-MD.com but it never made money so we eventually closed it down. We gave free, general psychiatric information all over the world, during early stages of the Internet. As an intern, my first wife took me on a date to an autopsy performed by her friend. My third wife use to sign up as the onsite doctor at Lincoln Center ballet and twice she couldn't make it. Guess who took her place. I still feel glad nobody broke a leg those nights.

Enjoy these stories. I did. I hope all you Hot Shots out there can use this story as a comparison on how to live a full life while dodging all the rip offs. You can send in your own stores for Volume 2 of True Great

Hot Stories. We will try to turn them into books, movies, TV series, Broadway plays, etc. Tell only the truth, as I did, to protect yourself against getting sued for libel. I hope to put all or parts of this book and the following versions into movies. Let's talk. We will monitor for your communication the email address listed below during many, many years to come.

Hot Shots, contact me with your ideas:
nedcruey@gmail.com
(702) 219-4584

KAREN RUSKIN, M.D.

My favorite combination: medical doctor and actress. We
were set up by a mutual friend, our accountant.
I once saw her in an off-Broadway production

Our wedding day at the
United Nations chapel
November 10, 1996

White water rafting in Alaska
1997

My wife, the scuba diver, on our honeymoon
February 1997

Hospital housing
Just before we
moved away to
Las Vegas

At the Galapagos, a trip
while in transit from NYC
to Las Vegas
January 1998

Arrived in Las Vegas from NYC
1/30/1998

Photo Caption for First Night in Vegas 1998

Our first night together as Las Vegas residents, on Karen's birthday, at Nero's (which later became The Homestead) at Caesar's Palace January 30, 1998

January 1999
with our newborn twins
Charles and Kenneth

On the balcony of
the Cary Grant Suite at
The Warwick with
our nanny
1999

Photo caption for babies and Mom
1999
Babies Kenneth and Charles,
just months old, with their mom
1999

Capital of Cambodia
2000
Phnom Penh

Famous hotel in Phuket, Thailand. After Scuba diving all day, we went in
the ocean from the beach, with no undertow warning and both almost
drowned. a lifeguard from the adjacent hotel threw a rope and saved us.
2000

Ayers Rock,
Austria
2000

Christmas
2002

Grandparents with
the twins at The
Meadows Pre-school

The Oracle of Delfi, Greece
during the Olympics
2004

Karen at
Athens
Olympics
2004

Family on the first Christmas
cruise of the Queen Mary 2
to the Caribbean
2004

Christmas on the Queen Mary
2004

Round the World Trip

Thailand
Round the World Trip
2005

In Northern Thailand
on our
Trip Around the World
2005

Tokyo Bay
on our
Trip Around the World
2005

Vladavostic, Russia
on the
Round the World trip
Transiberian Railroad

Geraldo Rivera interviewed me at the World Series of Poker at Binion's Horseshoe, Las Vegas, *circa* 2006.

Because of Geraldo Rivera's interview and because I knocked him out of that game, Michael Konik, in his book "The Man with $100,000 Breasts and Other Gambling Stories," devoted the last 90 pages of that book to poker tales about me as "Taxi Ned." Ten years before, he and I played private home poker games in Manhattan.

At the medical convention
in Havana
2006

National Hotel
Havana, Cuba

My only Smoking
experience

A non-smoker picture for
effect

My oil trucking business I sold just before the latest crash about 2014.

Trucks and the twins at age 9

Kenneth Cruey Summer Camp in
Colorado

Charles on the Colorado River

Charles in Pop Warner Football

Charles in front of Paris
Louvre Museum

We found this
exact replica of
my motorcycle
from my 1966
motorcycle trip

Our twins, age 12, at the
bluff at Lake McCarroll
Sault Ste Marie, Ontario

My summer home in the
late 1950's

Omaha Beach

2015 Christmas Cruise to the
Caribbean on the Queen Mary 2

SPACE CENTER
HOUSTON
NASA
June 18, 2013

Trump's Nevada victory speech

Our backyard during the Trump
Election Help/Thank You Barbecue

Our Las Vegas backyard
2016

Photo Caption for Turkish family circa 2012

Photo taken from the Internet *circa* 2012. Bottom row, from left: Maternal grandmother of my children, Eric and Lara, disbarred Turkish lawyer, fought me to deprive me any visitation with my children in the Ankara court in Turkey, lost, and then told me that my children had moved to Germany. Second from left, my daughter Lara, a student at Tulane University. Third from left, my son Eric, admitted to Yale but went to a minor college under full scholarship rather than ask me for money for school

Second row, between the maternal grandmother and Lara: Eric and Lara's mother, Ayse. Second row between Lara and Eric, Ayse's sister: I took her from her U. S. Citizenship ceremony to JFK Airport with her new American passport. To my knowledge, she has not returned to the USA since. She told me falsely in July 1999 that Eric, Lara, and their mother had moved to Izmir, Turkey.

Third row, third person from the left: Ayse's brother, a nice guy, who apologized on behalf of his family and all Turkish people for Ayse's behavior. He told me that she had worse behavior before she came to America

GREAT HOT SHOT STORIES
VOLUME 1
by Ned F. Cruey

<u>Favorite Quotes</u>:

May you live in interesting times

Improving the world "one complaint at a time" instead of "one compliment at a time"

If you are not making any mistakes, you are not going fast enough

Always work hard and work for yourself

KEEP EXPANDING YOUR MIND

Always keep a positive attitude

Can one get sued for libel for making true statements?

Better to live one day as a lion than 100 years as a sheep

We have limited time — make smart decisions

Never underestimate the power of blond hair

Happiness — having someone to look forward to

Good enough for government work

I want it all and I want it now

Looking at modern inventions makes me wish I had invented some of them

First words and life-long motto: "Car Car Go Go Bye Bye" — It has gotten me to 150 countries so far.

CPSIA information can be obtained
at www.ICGtesting.com
Printed in the USA
LVOW06*1055230916

505711LV00008B/10/P